THE AWAKENING

Friedrich Zuendel

THE AWAKENING

ONE MAN'S

BATTLE WITH

DARKNESS

THE PLOUGH PUBLISHNG HOUSE

The Awakening is based on three chapters
("Der Kampf," "Die Bussbewegung," and "Die Wunder")
from Friedrich Zuendel's biography
Johann Christoph Blumhardt, Zürich, Verlag S. Höhr, 1880.
The introduction is an abridged translation
of an article by Günter Krüger,
"Johann Christoph Blumhardt: Eine Reich-Gottes-Gestalt,"
in *Freundesbrief der Offensive Junger Christen*
No. 131, March-April 91/2, 59–73.
Used with permission.

Front Cover Photograph: © Eric Rank/Photonica
Back Cover Photograph: Bruderhof Archives.
Möttlingen at sunset, with Blumhardt's rectory
(white house) and parish church.

A catalog record for this book
is available from the British Library.

Library of Congress Cataloging-in-Publication Data

Zuendel, Friedrich.
  The awakening : one man's battle with darkness / Friedrich Zuendel.
    p. cm.
  The awakening is abridged from Freidrich Zündel's biography, Johann
    Christoph Blumhardt.
  ISBN 0-87486-982-X
  1. Blumhardt, Johann Christoph, 1805–1880. 2. Lutheran
Church—Germany—Clergy—Biography. I. Zündel, Friedrich. Johann Christoph
Blumhardt. II. Title.

BX8080.B615 Z82 2000
284.1'092—dc21
[B]
                                              99-054957

Printed in the USA

CONTENTS

According to oral tradition, the words on the plaque opposite mysteriously appeared, painted, on a shutter of Gottliebin Dittus's house in the village of Möttlingen during her fight against demonic powers, 1841–1843. The plaque itself, which was made later, still hangs on the house. The text reads:

Mensch: bedenk die Ewigkeit,
und spotte nicht der Gnadenzeit,
denn das Gericht ist nicht mehr weit.

Man: think on eternity,
and do not mock the time of grace,
for judgment is not far off.

PREFACE

Though relatively unknown to American readers, Johann Christoph Blumhardt (1805–1880) is widely recognized in his native Germany, perhaps because of his landmark biography, which appeared the year he died and still remains in print. The terrifying psychic phenomena described in it catapulted his parish into the public eye and still draw streams of curious visitors to it, one hundred and fifty years later.

The central fact of Blumhardt's life, however, was not his involvement in demonic struggle as such, but the childlike faith that led him into it – namely, his belief in the reality of the age-old battle between good and evil, and in a Jesus who was not only an historical figure, but a living reality whose cosmic power can be felt and experienced still today.

This faith embarrassed Blumhardt's contemporaries, so much so that his nervous superiors tried to suppress him by restricting his pastoral work. It is even more suspect in our time, when scientific progress has rendered rationalism the only acceptable faith for thinking people, and the untidy mysteries of the supernatural are relegated to talk shows and fiction shelves. Mention God, or Satan, and you're sure to evoke winces or worse.

For Blumhardt, there was no question about it: good and evil truly did exist, and not only in the abstract. To him, the well-known accounts of New Testament writers had meaning not only as parables or stories, but as factual instances of divine intervention in the lives of real men and women. To him, it seemed obvious that if demons were driven out, the sick healed, and the dead raised two thousand years ago, they could also be driven out, healed, and raised in the present too.

Zuendel's account is fascinating on an historical level, but it has vital implications for today's reader. And though the quiet pastor at the heart of the struggle he describes worried that it might become a source of exaggerated rumors, he would still want it to be discovered and grappled with and read. More than that, he would surely want it to give courage to those who despair over the spiritual emptiness of our church-filled landscapes, and hope to those whose hearts are open to believe.

The Editors
October 1999

I OVERVIEW

When Johann Christoph Blumhardt is discussed, opinions tend to polarize. Theologian Rudolf Bultmann writes, "I detest those Blumhardt stories!" whereas Walter Nigg says that in his opinion, Blumhardt was a saint: "If Blumhardt were really known to theologians – not just mentioned in passing, but understood – the whole business of theology in the universities would blow sky high."

What are these "Blumhardt stories," loathed by some but cherished as stirring evidence of God's power by others? Who was this man, whose unshakable convictions regarding the battle between good and evil continue to challenge the complacency of so many today, more than a century after his death?

Born in Stuttgart, Germany, to a long line of Swabian craftsmen, Johann Christoph Blumhardt (1805–1880) read the entire Bible twice by the time he was twelve, and the rest of his life bore the imprint of its message. Though his early devotion never faltered, he began to wonder even in his youth why the power of the gospel seemed so limited in the present day. If the Bible was truly the living word of God, he wondered, why was God's nearness so hard to perceive in the world around him? Where was the spirit that had animated the first believers in the apostolic era?

Later, at Tübingen, Blumhardt studied theology, philosophy, history, mathematics, and other subjects. After receiving his university degree, he spent six years teaching in Basel, Switzerland (where he met his future wife, Doris Köllner) and then returned to Germany, where he took up the position of curate in the town of Iptingen.

Iptingen was deemed the most difficult parish in the region. Divided by dissension, the congregation was also at odds with its youth and long out of touch with its aging, eccentric minister, whom Blumhardt had come to replace. Luckily Blumhardt's ability to draw out the best in people and to inspire trust in them stood him in good stead, and he soon won the hearts of his parishioners, even though he was cautious at first. Sermons provided the key to many a locked door. After funerals or weddings, enthusiastic listeners would spread the word, and the following Sunday, newcomers would show up in the pews. Though many were from the immediate vicinity, crowds soon began to come from farther away. In a letter Blumhardt wrote to his fiancée, we read:

> Yesterday I heard – and it aroused all kinds of painful emotions in me – that a neighboring pastor recently broke into tears in the pulpit. Almost fifty people from his congregation come to hear me each Sunday, neglecting him for an unfamiliar preacher. You can imagine how deeply this upsets me, for I can easily put myself in the position of

such a man. But what can be done about it? I never invite these people, and I take great pains not to give them occasion to accuse me of seeking a following…I am thinking of paying the good pastor a visit very soon.

As Blumhardt's temporary appointment at Iptingen neared its end, anxious parishioners tried to talk him out of leaving. Concerned that Doris had something to do with the move, they voiced their fears that she might distract him from the path of faith. Blumhardt listened with friendly good humor and then reassured them that he would take their concern to heart. Writing to Doris that she must take care not to let their upcoming marriage and family life jeopardize his calling to the ministry, he told her, "What I fear most is gradually sliding into a rut and forfeiting the Spirit from above."

In the summer of 1838 Blumhardt, now thirty-three, left Iptingen and took on the pastorate at nearby Möttlingen. He and Doris were married shortly afterwards.

Möttlingen and its affiliated parish, Haugstett, lie at the north end of the Black Forest – both villages were among the poorest in the region. When Blumhardt arrived, a crippling spiritual lethargy lay over the whole congregation. Pastor Barth, Blumhardt's immediate predecessor and a brilliant preacher, complained bitterly to him that the parish seemed preached to death; people were fed up with the gospel, and if some still attended church, most of them slept in their seats. The entire town seemed to be held in a sleepy thrall.

Beginning in the fall of 1841, Blumhardt was drawn into a spiritual struggle, which he referred to for the rest of his life as "the fight." At first, he tried to keep a cautious distance from it, but it soon became obvious that he would not be able to stay uninvolved.

Gottliebin Dittus, a young woman from a pious Möttlingen family who had once been Pastor Barth's favorite pupil, was regarded in her village as a "God-fearing" member of the parish. At the same time she was known, ever since her childhood, to have suffered recurring nervous disorders and various other maladies, including inexplicable "attacks" not unlike epileptic seizures.

Repulsed by her peculiar behavior, Blumhardt kept his distance from her. He would come when summoned during her worst attacks, but in general he felt that her case was no task for him as a pastor. Village physician Dr. Späth, on the other hand, felt that Gottliebin's disorders were beyond the scope of his medical knowledge, if not symptomatic of supernatural forces at work.

Blumhardt's friends advised him to distance himself from her, yet he could not be dissuaded from his involvement. For one thing, he was ashamed at the thought of conceding power to the darkness affecting her. Moreover, he pitied her. Little did he know that he had embarked on an uncharted spiritual journey that would last for the next two years. Taking the form of intense prayers and of terrifyingly real dialogues with demons that spoke through Gottliebin, this battle would demand all of Blumhardt's energies.

Meanwhile, similar symptoms appeared in Gottliebin's sister Katharina, who suffered to such an extent that during the last and most dramatic phase of Blumhardt's fight, his energies were concentrated almost entirely on her. Around two in the morning on the final night, a demonic voice howled, "Jesus is the victor! Jesus is the victor!" With that, the two-year-long struggle came to an end, and both women were restored to complete health.

"Jesus is the victor!" That loud cry was heard throughout the village, and its echoes reverberated for the rest of Blumhardt's life – in his thinking, his preaching, and his pastoral work. And yet, whenever he would later be asked about the fight in Möttlingen, he played it down, insisting that it was not the battle itself, but what came afterwards, that was really significant.

By Easter 1844 the entire town was swept up in an unprecedented movement of repentance and revival. The awakening spread beyond the town, too, into neighboring villages and farther afield in the Black Forest. As time went on, the movement spread so wide that worship services at Möttlingen were regularly swamped by outsiders. On Good Friday

1845, for instance, visitors from 176 towns and villages were counted.

The working of the Spirit at Möttlingen was visible in concrete ways: at Sunday services, for instance, residents offered their pews to visitors, seating themselves in the churchyard. In the same way they placed their houses, their beds, and their tables at the disposal of one flood of guests after another with unheard-of hospitality.

Following the revival, and almost as a side effect, people began to be healed from various physical afflictions. Some of the healings took place as early as the winter of 1844, seemingly as a result of confession, and without having been prayed for. In every case, Blumhardt only heard about it afterwards. Soon, however, word spread, and growing numbers of people came to him seeking bodily healing through prayer.

Numerous cases of spiritual and physical healing were reported during this period, yet they were never the focal point of Blumhardt's interest. For the most part they happened incidentally and were not sensationalized, but looked on as a natural outcome of the awakening in the church. There were those who regarded Blumhardt as a miracle-worker, but he energetically dismissed the idea. As he put it, he could only pray, "Jesus, help!" – and anyone who believed in Jesus could do that. He insisted that credit belonged to no one but God.

Blumhardt was never interested in purely physical healing; that, he felt, was a medical concern. Nor did he see himself as a competitor to the local doctor, whom he continued to encourage his congregation to use. His concern was always the healing of the whole person: "If someone desires physical health but does not simultaneously experience forgiveness for his sins, it won't help him much to make him healthy." When Blumhardt did take a particular interest in a case of illness, it was because the doctors had reached their limits. Even then, Blumhardt's prayers for healing were not always followed by a cure. Contemporary accounts mention many permanent cures of serious illness, but they also report sicknesses that were not cured. Among some patients, temporary improvement was followed by reversal.

In his interpretation of these happenings, Blumhardt came to two conclusions: first, that Christianity had lost its full authority both to free souls and to heal them; second, that it was guilty of this loss. According to God's original plan, a servant of God should also be the bearer of divine gifts and powers; he should be empowered not only with the gift of preaching, but with the gift of healing and freeing. Yet as Blumhardt lamented, "Christianity knows absolutely nothing of this anymore."

Meanwhile the pastor was becoming a problem for both government and church officials. As early as January 1846 the regional government, worried that

Blumhardt was undermining local professional practices, forbade him to include healing as part of his pastoral office and demanded he call on a doctor instead. Church authorities used the same argument. Advising Blumhardt that the role of religion was to provide comfort by emphasizing patience and the blessings brought by suffering, they forbade him to take overnight guests in his home. Later they even barred him from receiving out-of-town visitors in his house – for instance, after Sunday services.

During the following summer, perhaps (Blumhardt wondered) because of the strenuous labor that marked daily life in Möttlingen, the spiritual awakening began to ebb. Villagers still gathered for daily devotions, but they came in dwindling numbers, and there was growing apathy and a sense of inertia that disquieted Blumhardt. Determined not to let the parish slide back into old ruts, he attempted to spur on his congregation. His preaching became more forceful, and his pastoral clarity sharper – not only toward his listeners, but also toward himself. As he later wrote:

> Many weaknesses of human nature – weaknesses one might hardly take into account, but which have deep significance if our Christianity is not to consist of mere fragments – became apparent to me. I recognized such weaknesses in myself first, and following an inner urge, confessed them to one of my colleagues. I felt humbled by my shortcomings –

omissions, stupidities, and bad habits – and from then on I sat on the same bench with my congregation. I did this by bringing my failings before them, and the result was the emergence of a new movement of repentance and humility. Once more my parishioners searched their souls and, for the most part, sought me out again.

It should be noted – especially today, when there is a wealth of theories on how to revitalize dying churches – that Blumhardt had no such strategies at hand. He applied himself vigorously in rebuilding his parish, yet he always maintained that the master builder was God. He also observed something seldom mentioned today in discussions of spiritual renewal: the problem of believers who, though respectable and sincerely committed, are influenced or even bound by forces of darkness. In retrospect, he noted that these forces presented the greatest obstacle to renewal in his parish. As long as the reality of satanic power was not recognized, exposed, and done away with in every corner, the suffocating spiritual fog that hung over the church would not lift.

––––––––

Modern minds tend to deny or ignore the very existence of satanic forces, let alone their hold on specific individuals. Blumhardt felt that this skepticism trivializes the reality of evil. He argued that every human being has demons of his or her own to fight, that all are affected in some way by the power of evil.

> As soon as one tells a bible story with a phrase like "Then he cast out the demon…" people tune out; they dismiss it as religious nonsense. They do this because they cannot recognize any capacity for evil, any wretchedness in themselves.

> If we are not aware of human wretchedness, we cannot appreciate the Savior's role in the kingdom of God, which means the end for Satan…And it will come to that! If we already have power to overcome evil, is that not enough reason to believe that God is beginning to take up his reign?

Blumhardt's insights have great relevance today, when interest (and involvement) in pagan religions, the occult, satanism, and New Age philosophy is at an unprecedented high. So does his recognition that in fighting for clarity in any of these areas, scientific or psychological literature is of little help; even if informative, it does not take evil seriously and is therefore unable to inspire action against it. For Blumhardt, the only acceptable tools were the "pure weapons of prayer and the word of God."

The building up of the church in Möttlingen did not begin with preaching but, as Blumhardt put it, with struggle, prayer, and finally, victory over "personalities of darkness." He never belittled the role of evangelization, but sought to draw attention also to what blocks (rather than spurs on) God's reign.

Contrary to popular belief, Blumhardt was (he claimed) only an accompanist to the fight in Möttlingen, and not its driving force. After it was over, it seemed as if an invisible sluice had been opened: suddenly, people came to repentance quite on their own, and in their new faith they found that prayer could relieve their mental and physical sufferings. There came into being, as Blumhardt's son Christoph later put it, "a church aflame with the first love."

As the revival at Möttlingen continued, house churches sprang up throughout the vicinity, and what started as a trickle of people seeking Blumhardt's help became a flood. Blumhardt's fame had spread so far he had even begun to receive offers and inquiries from abroad. Eventually, the pastor decided to leave Möttlingen. There were several reasons for this: the insufficient size of the vicarage, restrictions placed on him by nervous church and state authorities, and lastly the incompatibility of his pastoral duties with the demands of speaking engagements and other activities that took him away from his congregation.

After some searching Blumhardt was able, with the generous help of friends and benefactors, to buy an unprofitable spa with sulfur springs in Bad Boll, a village not far way. Here he moved in the summer of 1852 with his family and four members of the Dittus family, loyal friends ever since Gottlieben's healing almost ten years earlier.

At Bad Boll, Blumhardt was allowed to remain a pastor in the state church, and though he received no stipend, he was permitted to carry out all pastoral functions – baptisms, communions, confirmations, weddings and funerals. On top of this, the spa was designated a special parish, and the restrictions imposed on Blumhardt in Möttlingen were lifted.

Bad Boll had its own personnel to be integrated into the pastor's household, and in addition the guests who had formerly flocked to Möttlingen now sought out Blumhardt at his new residence. Sometimes there were 120 to 150 guests staying in the house at one time. Not surprisingly, the conduct of these visitors sometimes clashed with that of the community gathered around Blumhardt, even though he tried to preserve the ambience of an informal extended household. Difficulties arose with the staff, too. Describing how he dealt with them, his biographer later wrote:

> Blumhardt employed many people out of compassion, and firing them was not his strong point. The conduct of several of the staff members was questionable, however. At one point, when one instance of hidden immorality after another had come to his attention, he grew distraught and said to his wife and children, "All of us must repent." Days of ear-

nest self-examination followed, awakening new zeal for prayer and Bible study throughout the house. Before long, one employee after the other came quietly of his own accord to Blumhardt's room to confess his sins, and a movement similar to that at Möttlingen stirred through the entire staff.

Under Blumhardt's direction, Bad Boll soon exerted a magnetic attraction quite different from that of the former spa. People came from all over Germany and from foreign countries. All of them, whether believers or nonbelievers, were welcomed with the same cordiality. Class distinctions of the era were still taken into account (though not as formally observed as elsewhere), but they were soon bridged by the communal living arrangements of the household. At mealtimes princesses and peasants, scholars and uneducated laborers, Germans and foreigners sat next to each other at the same table. According to those present, it was a foretaste of the great banquet of nations in the kingdom of God. A letter from historian Karl von Hase, a guest, offers a firsthand description:

> You may be told that it smacks of sectarianism, but I assure you that in everything Blumhardt sets in motion there is not a trace of unhealthiness or false pietism. A fresh, joyful spirit blows through this house and permeates the outer life as well as the inner; it gives one a living impression of the peace of God – a peace beyond all reason. It is an atmosphere that works on the soul like a mountain

breeze on the body. As long as you are immersed in it, you believe it cannot be otherwise. All that is holy is so human, and all that is human so transfigured, and all without coercion.

Large as it had become, the household remained a family. Mornings began with a worship meeting for the staff, led by Blumhardt. The entire household then met for breakfast with all the guests, after which Blumhardt held another meeting, much like the evening devotions he held at the end of dinner. After the noon and evening meal, he would remain seated with his guests, cigar in hand. Here he was ready to discuss any question presented to him, and just as ready to listen and learn. He showed great interest in personal concerns, even mundane ones; all the same, he tried to set them in their proper perspective by helping his listeners to see them in the light of God's greatness.

Blumhardt's style of preaching was generally empty of pathos and bore no trace of pulpit oratory. He admitted, "The fuller my heart, the drier my words seem." People who met him for the first time were usually surprised by his unimposing manner. One guest said of him, "He has absolutely no self-importance, and there is nothing extraordinary about conversing with him. He has a good sense of humor and even comes out with an earthy joke now and then." All the same, Blumhardt could be curt, even harsh, when occasion demanded. He could discern where sensitivity and caring patience were necessary, but also where brevity and sharpness were required.

Countless instances of healing took place at Bad Boll; they seemed to be such a regular outcome of God's presence in this spirit-filled family that there were always people at the table who had been freed or healed. But Blumhardt, worried that people might begin to seek him out solely in order to be cured of physical ailments, was adamant that no fuss should be made over such occurrences. He vehemently opposed all attempts to isolate the gift of healing from other gifts of the Spirit, and when he felt medical treatment was appropriate, he referred an invalid to a doctor.

All in all, Blumhardt's attitude toward the reality of divine power was almost matter-of-fact. Had not Jesus said, "If I cast out demons through the Holy Spirit, then the kingdom of God has already come to you" (Matt. 12:28) and "The kingdom of God is already among you" (Luke 17:21)?

Still, Blumhardt never sat back, satisfied. To him, the fight, the awakening, and the miracles of healing that followed it were merely a tiny premonition of what is to come, like the first flash of lightning before a storm. Thus, despite all he had experienced, he continued to grieve all his life over the spiritual poverty of Christendom, and repeatedly lamented that "we no longer have the spirit of Pentecost." Distressed that Christians had lost their expectancy, he even saw a relationship between this lack and the delay of Christ's second coming. "How can the Lord wish to come to a people who no longer await his coming, a people for whom he has become a matter of indifference?"

On the other hand, he observed that where the second coming of Christ was still reckoned with, its expectation was frequently overshadowed by visions of apocalyptic horror and sullied by fear. Blumhardt had only one response for such anxiety. "I cannot believe that the Savior will come as a great destroyer," he would say. Again and again, he countered visions of end-time horror with his belief that Christ's judgment will be more liberating than terrifying – a setting straight rather than an act of devastation. "He is coming to reveal salvation, not doom; to reveal joy and peace, not horror and destruction...The sign of mourning that hangs over humankind shall be removed at last."

And when he spoke of humankind, he meant all of earth's people, not just some small flock of redeemed Christians: "I believe that Jesus, the friend of man, will reveal a compassion so great that many wicked people will be saved."

Still, Blumhardt saw the kingdom of God as a state from which all forces hostile to God would be banished in the aggressive battle that must be fought against "the prince of this world." The church,

Blumhardt said, must take part in this offensive and to do so successfully it must call on divine authority.

If Blumhardt is right, it follows that the Christian's life must take on the character of a war. Today the church does not face merely one possessed woman, but a world infected and overrun with demons in the most varied spheres – politics, technology, economics, academia, religion, and art. And unless we recognize and identify these demons, the spheres under their sway can not serve the cause of God.

For followers of Jesus, then, the challenge is to take leave of all spiritual pacifism, all egotistical and self-centered private piety. It means mobilizing and taking to the front lines. Finally, it means living in such a way that only God rules. As Blumhardt never tired of pointing out, Christ's central command sums up his will for his disciples, "As I have loved you, so you are to love one another" (John 13:35). This same command is spelled out in Jesus' prayer for his disciples (John 17:23): "May they be one, as we are one; I in them and you in me; may they be perfectly one. Then the world will know that you sent me."

Günter Krüger

II THE FIGHT

On July 31, 1838, the people of Möttlingen, a small town in southern Germany, turned out to welcome their new pastor. A zealous thirty-three-year-old, Johann Christoph Blumhardt had spent years preparing for such a position, and was looking forward to serving his new flock as a minister, teacher, and counselor. Now, finally, he and his fiancée Doris Köllner could marry, settle down, and raise a family.

Blumhardt could never have anticipated the events he was about to be thrust into. Through them, the power of God to which he clung came close to him with a vividness experienced by only a few throughout history. At the request of his ecclesiastical superiors, he recounted these events in a detailed report entitled *An Account of Gottliebin Dittus' Illness.* In his own memory the events lived on as "the fight."

Before long, completely against Blumhardt's wish, a distorted version of his report began to circulate publicly. This compelled Blumhardt, who had not even kept the original, to publish a carefully edited second version. He made one hundred copies and stated in the preface that he did not wish to see it circulated further.

Out of respect for that wish, the following account describes manifestations of supernatural forces only where necessary to demonstrate God's victories over them. However, general, mysterious hints would envelop his struggle in an apocryphal twilight. Besides, Blumhardt regarded his experiences during the fight as so significant for the church and for the world that he would almost certainly agree to making their essential content public now. In a sense, we owe it to him to do so.

In the preface to his report Blumhardt wrote:

Until now I have never spoken with such boldness and candor to anybody about my experiences. Even my best friends look at me askance and act as though they feel threatened by even hearing about these things. Until now, most of it has remained a secret that I could have taken with me to the grave. It would have been easy to give an account that avoided offending any reader, but I could not do that. At almost every paragraph I asked myself if it was not rash to tell everything just as it was, but time and again an inner voice would say, "Out with it!"

So I dared it, in the name of Jesus, the victor. This is an honest report of what I can still remember, and I am firmly convinced that the Lord will hold his hand over me in this. My only intention is to tell everything to the honor of him who is the victor over all dark powers. I cannot take it amiss if somebody is mistrustful of these accounts, for these things are beyond our understanding. They are, however, based on observations and experiences over nearly two years, ones which can in every case be corroborated by eye-witnesses.

In speaking out unreservedly for the first time, I ask that the information given here be regarded as private, as when close friends share a secret. I also ask the reader to be so good as to read the whole report several times before forming a judgment. Meanwhile, I put my trust in Him who has human hearts in his power. Whatever the verdict of those who read this account, I rest assured in the knowledge that I have spoken the unvarnished truth, and in the rock-like certainty that Jesus is the victor.

Möttlingen, a parish at the northern end of the Black Forest which numbered 874 souls when Blumhardt arrived, encompasses two villages. Möttlingen proper, with a population of 535, overlooks the Nagold River and has the architecture, costumes, and customs of the Swabian lowland. Haugstett, the parish branch, is more typical of the Black Forest region, and its inhabitants were known at the time for a spirit of independence so fierce that it often bordered on hostility toward their pastor.

Near the edge of the village of Möttlingen stands a ramshackle house, recognizable now just as it was then by a window shutter bearing this weather-worn inscription:

Man, think on eternity,
And do not mock the time of grace,
For judgment is not far off.

In the spring of 1840 a poor family by the name of Dittus, consisting of two brothers and three sisters, moved into the ground floor apartment of this house. The eldest, Andreas, later became a village councilor. Then came Johann Georg, half blind and known as Hans. After him came three girls: Katharina, Anna Maria, and Gottliebin, who was born October 13, 1815. Their parents, both devout Christians, had died young.

Gottliebin was spiritually precocious and a favorite pupil of Pastor Barth, Blumhardt's predecessor. Adept at composing verse, she later wrote many fine songs. Yet from childhood on she experienced uncanny things, and contracted one strange illness after the next, which more than once forced her to give up a good job. Though no one was certain of the cause of these afflictions, they were presumed to spring from her involvement in the magic practices rampant in rural German villages of the era. Barth used his connections to consult eminent physicians on her behalf, and she recovered fairly well from her last ailment, a kidney disease.

Gottliebin felt as attracted to Blumhardt as she felt repelled by him. At his first sermon she had to fight a desire to scratch his eyes out. On the other hand, Blumhardt could be sure of seeing her wherever she had a chance of hearing an uplifting word from him. For instance, she attended his service at the remote parish branch of Haugstett every week, even though one of her legs was shorter than the other, and it was difficult for her to walk long distances. She had a marked, dejected sort of shyness, which, when broken, revealed a defensive reserve. She made a downright unpleasant impression on Blumhardt and on others as well.

No sooner had the Dittuses moved into their new apartment than Gottliebin reported seeing and hearing strange things in the house. Other family members noticed them, too. On the first day, as Andreas said grace at table, Gottliebin fell unconscious to the floor at the words "Come, Lord Jesus, be our guest." Then in the bedroom, sitting room, and kitchen her siblings heard recurring banging and shuffling, which terrified them and upset the people living upstairs.

Other peculiar things happened too. At night, for instance, Gottliebin would feel her hands forcibly placed one above the other. She had visions of figures, small lights, and other things and her behavior became gradually more repulsive and inexplicable. Yet because no one was greatly concerned about the "poor orphan family," and because Gottliebin kept quiet about her experiences, most people ignored it. Blumhardt heard rumors about the matter, but he took no notice of them.

Finally, in the fall of 1841, when her nightly torments became unbearable, Gottliebin came to Blumhardt in his rectory. Voluntarily confessing various things from her past, she seemed to hope that confession would relieve her trials. Yet she spoke in such general terms that Blumhardt could not say much to help her.

From December 1841 through the following February Gottliebin suffered from erysipelas of the face and lay dangerously ill. Blumhardt did not visit her often however, as he was annoyed by her behavior. As soon as she caught sight of him, she would look to one side. When he greeted her, she would not reply. When he prayed, she would separate her previously folded hands. Though before and after his visits she acted fine, she paid no attention to his words and seemed almost unconscious when he was there. At the time, Blumhardt regarded her as self-willed and spiritually proud, and decided to stay away rather than expose himself to embarrassment.

Gottliebin did have a faithful friend and adviser in her physician, Dr. Späth and she poured out everything, including her spooky experiences, to him. Dr. Späth was unable to cure her strangest ailment – breast bleeding – but later, when Blumhardt took her into his care, it vanished, though he was informed of the complaint and its cure only later.

Not until April 1842, after the mysterious happenings had gone on for more than two years, did Blumhardt learn more details from the tormented woman's relatives, who came to him for advice. They were desperate, for the banging noises that echoed through the house at night had become so loud they could be heard all over the neighborhood. Furthermore, Gottliebin had begun to receive visits from an apparition. The figure resembled a woman who had died two years before, and carried a dead child in her arms. Gottliebin claimed that this woman (whose name she only divulged later) always stood at a certain spot before her bed. At times the woman would move toward her and say repeatedly, "I just want to find rest," or, "Give me a paper, and I won't come again," or something of the sort. As Blumhardt reported:

> The Dittus family asked me if it would be all right to find out more by questioning the apparition. My advice was that Gottliebin should on no account enter into conversation with it; there was no knowing how much might be her self-deception. It was certain, I said, that people can be sucked into a bottomless quagmire when they become involved with spiritualism. Gottliebin should pray earnestly and trustingly; then the whole thing would peter out of its own accord.
>
> As one of her sisters was away in domestic service and her brother wasn't home much, I asked a woman friend of hers to sleep with her to help take her mind off these things if possible. But she was so disturbed by the banging that she helped Gottliebin investigate the matter. At length, guided by a glimmer of light, they discovered behind a board above

the bedroom entrance half a sheet of paper with
writing on it, so smeared with soot that it was unde-
cipherable. Beside it they found three crowns – one
of them minted in 1828 – and various bits of paper,
also covered with soot.

From then on everything was quiet. "The spook
business has come to an end," Blumhardt wrote to
Barth. Two weeks later, though, the thumping
started again. By the light of a flicker of flame from
the stove, the family found more such objects, as
well as various powders. An analysis by the district
physician and an apothecary in nearby Calw proved
inconclusive.

Meanwhile, the banging increased; it went on day
and night and reached a peak whenever Gottliebin
was in the room. Along with some others who were
curious, Dr. Späth twice stayed in the apartment
overnight, and found it worse than he had expected.
The affair became more and more of a sensation, affecting the surrounding countryside and drawing
tourists from farther away. In an attempt to put an
end to the scandal, Blumhardt decided to undertake
a thorough investigation himself. With the mayor
Kraushaar (a carpet manufacturer known for his
level-headedness) and a half dozen village council-
ors, Blumhardt made secret arrangements for an in-
spection during the night of June 9, 1842. In advance
he sent Mose Stanger, a young married man related
to Gottliebin who later became Blumhardt's most

faithful supporter. The others followed at about ten o'clock in the evening, posting themselves in pairs in and around the house.

As Blumhardt entered the house, he was met by two powerful bangs from the bedroom, followed by several more. He heard all sorts of bangs and knocks, mostly in the bedroom, where Gottliebin lay fully clothed on the bed. The other observers out-side and on the floor above heard it all. After a while they all gathered in the ground floor apartment, convinced that what they heard must originate there. The tumult seemed to grow, especially when Blumhardt suggested a verse from a hymn and spoke a few words of prayer. Within three hours they heard the sound of twenty-five blows, directed at a certain spot in the bedroom. These were powerful enough to cause a chair to jump, the windows to clatter, and sand to trickle from the ceiling. People living at a distance were reminded of New Year's Eve firecrackers. At the same time there were other noises of varying volume, like a light drumming of fingertips or a more or less regular tapping. The sounds seemed to come mainly from beneath the bed, though a search revealed nothing. They did no-tice, though, that the bangs in the bedroom were loudest when everybody was in the sitting room. Blumhardt reported:

> Finally, at about one o'clock, while we were all in the living room, Gottliebin called me to her and said

she could hear the shuffling sound of an approaching apparition. Then she asked me if, once she saw
it, I would permit her to identify it. I refused. By that
time I had heard more than enough and did not
want to run the risk of having many people see
things that could not be explained. I declared the
investigation over, asked Gottliebin to get up, saw
to it that she found accommodation in another
house, and left. Gottliebin's brother Hans told us
later that he still saw and heard various things after
our departure.

The next day, a Friday, there was a church service.
Afterward, Gottliebin went to visit her old home.
Half an hour later a large crowd had gathered in
front of the house, and a messenger notified Blumhardt that Gottliebin was unconscious and close to
death. He hurried there and found her lying on the
bed, completely rigid, her head burning hot and her
arms trembling. She seemed to be suffocating. The
room was crammed with people, including a doctor
from a neighboring village who happened to be in
Möttlingen and had rushed to the spot. He tried
various things to revive Gottliebin but went away
shaking his head. Half an hour later she came to. She
confided to Blumhardt that she had again seen the
figure of the woman with the dead child and had
fallen to the floor unconscious.

Another search of the place that afternoon turned
up a number of strange objects apparently con-

nected with sorcery – including tiny bones. Blum-hardt, accompanied by the mayor, took them to a specialist, who identified them as bird bones.

Wishing to quell the general hubbub, which was now getting out of hand, Blumhardt found new ac-commodations for Gottliebin, first with a female cousin and later with another cousin, Johann Georg Stanger (the father of Mose Stanger), who was a vil-lage councilor and Gottliebin's godfather. Blum-hardt advised Gottliebin not to enter her own house for the time being, and she agreed – in fact, she did not move back there until the following year. He also tried to prevent further commotion by advising her brother Hans not to visit her.

> I had a particular dread of manifestations of clair-voyance, which are often unpleasantly sensational. A mysterious and dangerous field had opened up before me, and I could only commit the matter to the Lord in my personal prayers, asking him to pro-tect me in every situation that might arise. When-ever the matter took a more serious turn, the mayor, Mose, and I would meet in my study to pray and talk, which kept us all in a sober frame of mind.
>
> I shall never forget the fervent prayers for wis-dom, strength, and help that those men sent up to God. Together we searched through the Bible, deter-mined not to go any further than Scripture led us. It never entered our minds to perform miracles, but it grieved us deeply to realize how much power the

devil still has over humankind. Our heartfelt compassion went out not only to the poor woman whose misery we saw before us, but to the millions who have turned away from God and become entangled in the secret snares of darkness. We cried to God, asking that at least in this case he would give us the victory and trample Satan underfoot.

It took weeks for the uproar in the area to die down. Complete strangers came and wanted to visit the house, some even wanting to spend a night in it to convince themselves that the rumors were true. But Blumhardt resolutely refused all such requests, including one made by three Catholic priests from nearby Baden, who wanted to spend several hours in the house at night. The house was placed under the watchful custody of the village policeman, who happened to live opposite it.

Gradually things quieted down, and most people in the village remained unaware of what followed, though occasionally this or that came to somebody's notice. As for his own congregation, Blumhardt later said, "Generally speaking, I met with earnest, reverent, and expectant sympathy throughout the fight, even if it was mostly unspoken. That made it much easier for me to hold out, while at the same time rendering it impossible for me to give up." Meanwhile the din in the house continued unabated and only ended a full two years later.

Before long, similar noises started in Gottliebin's new dwelling. Whenever they were heard, she would fall into violent convulsions that could last four or five hours. Once they were so violent that the bedstead was forced out of joint. Dr. Späth, who was present, said in tears, "The way this woman is left lying here, one would think there is no one in this village to care for souls in need!"

Blumhardt took up the challenge and began visiting Gottliebin more often:

> Her whole body shook; every muscle of her head and arms burned and trembled, or rattled, for they were individually rigid and stiff, and she foamed at the mouth. She had been lying in this state for several hours, and the doctor, who had never seen anything like it, was at his wits' end. Then suddenly she came to, sat up, and asked for a drink of water. One could scarcely believe it was the same person.

One day a traveling preacher acquainted with Gottliebin visited her and dropped in at the rectory. On taking leave, he raised a forefinger at Blumhardt and admonished him, "Do not forget your pastoral duty!"

"What am I to do?" thought Blumhardt. "I'm doing what any pastor does. What more can I do?"

Some time later, on a Sunday evening, Blumhardt visited the sick woman again. Several of her friends were present. Sitting some distance from her bed, he silently watched as she convulsed: twisting her arms, arcing her back in the most painful manner, and foaming at the mouth. Blumhardt continued:

> It became clear to me that something demonic was at work here, and I was pained that no remedy had been found for the horrible affair. As I pondered this, indignation seized me – I believe it was an inspiration from above. I walked purposefully over to Gottliebin and grasped her cramped hands. Then, trying to hold them together as best as possible (she was unconscious), I shouted into her ear, "Gottliebin, put your hands together and pray, 'Lord Jesus, help me!' We have seen enough of what the devil can do; now let us see what the Lord Jesus can do!" Moments later the convulsions ceased, and to the astonishment of those present, she woke up and repeated those words of prayer after me.
>
> This was the decisive moment, and it thrust me into the fight with irresistible force. I had acted on an impulse; it had never occurred to me what to do until then. But the impression that single impulse left on me stayed with me so clearly that later it was often my only reassurance, convincing me that what I had undertaken was not of my own choice or presumption. Of course at the time I could not possibly have imagined the horrible developments still to come.

Blumhardt only recognized the full significance of this turning point later on. He had turned deliberately and directly to God, and God had immediately begun to guide his actions. From this point on, Blumhardt was convinced that it was vital for the ultimate victory of God's kingdom that the kingdom of darkness and its influences suffer defeat here on earth. He also recognized more clearly the role of faith in the struggle between light and darkness. The depth to which divine redemption penetrates into human lives in this struggle, he saw, ultimately depends on the faith and expectation of its fighters.

Blumhardt explained what he saw as his own role in all this:

> At that time Jesus stood at the door and knocked, and I opened it to him. This is the call of Him who wants to come again: "Behold, I stand at the door; I am already waiting there. I want to come into your life, want to break into your 'reality' with the full power of grace given me by the Father, to prepare for my full return. I am knocking, but you are so engrossed in your possessions, your political quarrels, and theological wrangling, that you do not hear my voice."

Far from fully subsiding after Blumhardt's intervention, Gottliebin's illness soon resumed in earnest. Following this first breakthrough, the woman had several hours of peace, but at ten o'clock in the evening Blumhardt was called to her bedside again. Her convulsions had returned. Blumhardt asked her to pray aloud, "Lord Jesus, help me!" Once more, the convulsions ceased immediately, and when new attacks came Blumhardt frustrated them with the same prayer, until after three hours she was able to relax and exclaimed, "Now I feel quite well."

Gottliebin remained peaceful until nine o'clock the following evening, when Blumhardt called on her with two friends he brought along whenever he knew her to be alone. As they entered Gottliebin's room, she rushed at Blumhardt and tried to strike him, though she seemed unable to aim the blows effectively. After this, she plunked her hands down on the bed, and it seemed to those present as if some evil power came streaming out through her fingertips. It continued like this for some time, until finally the convulsions abated.

But before long, a new wave of distress engulfed Gottliebin. The sound of tapping fingers was once more around her, she received a sudden blow on her chest, and she once more caught sight of the apparition she had seen in her old home. This time she told Blumhardt who the figure was; it was a widow who had died two years before, a woman Blumhardt knew well. In her last days she had sighed a lot, and said she longed for peace but never found it. Once, when Blumhardt had quoted to her from a hymn, "Peace, the highest good of all," she had asked him for it and copied it. Later, on her deathbed, tormented by her conscience, she had confessed several heavy sins to Blumhardt, but it had not seemed to give her much peace. Blumhardt wrote:

When I got to Gottliebin, I heard the tapping. She lay quietly in bed. Suddenly it seemed as if something entered into her, and her whole body started to move. I said a few words of prayer and mentioned the name of Jesus. Immediately she began to roll her eyes, pulled her hands apart, and cried out in a voice not her own, either in accent or inflection, "I cannot bear that name!" We all shuddered. I had never yet heard anything like it, and in my heart I called on God to give me wisdom and prudence – and above all to preserve me from untimely curiosity. In the end, firmly resolved to limit myself to what was necessary and to let my intuition tell me if I went too far, I posed a few questions, addressing them to the voice, which I assumed belonged to the dead widow. The conversation went something like this:

"Is there no peace in the grave?"

"No."

"Why not?"

"It is the reward for my deeds."

"Have you not confessed everything?"

"No, I murdered two children and buried them in a field."

"Do you not know where to get help? Can you not pray?"

"I cannot pray."

"Do you not know Jesus who can forgive sins?"

"I cannot bear the sound of that name."

"Are you alone?"

"No."

"Who is with you?"

Hesitatingly, but then with a rush, the voice replied, "The most wicked of all."

The conversation went on like this for a while. The speaker accused herself of sorcery, on account of which she was bound to the devil. Seven times she had possessed someone and then left his or her body, she said. I asked her if I might pray for her, and after some hesitation she permitted me. When I finished, I told her she could not remain in Gottliebin's body. At first she seemed to plead with me, but then she became defiant. However, I commanded her to come out. At that, Gottliebin's hands fell forcefully to the bed, and her possession seemed to come to an end.

Along with his close friends the mayor and Mose Stanger, Blumhardt earnestly pondered whether or not he should enter into even a limited conversation with a spirit. The Bible always guided them in such considerations, particularly the passage starting at Luke 8:27. In light of his own experiences, Blumhardt offered the following thoughts on Luke's account of how Jesus healed the possessed Gergesene:

Luke reports that instead of departing immediately, as was usually the case, the demons voiced a request. They feared being sent into the abyss. Evidently, Jesus did not respond harshly. Having come to redeem the living and the dead to the widest extent possible, he, their future judge, could not stand there insensitive. Hence he showed himself approachable, and stopped to listen. He asked the unclean spirit, who was representing all the others, "What is your name?" He evidently put this question not to the possessed man, but to the spirit speaking out of him; he wanted to know what name the spirit had when alive.

Jesus was aware that demons, as departed human spirits, fear hell. By asking the demon's name – which he, being the Lord, would of course already know – he showed interest and compassion. This also suggests that he considered the demon to be human rather than non-human. The demon chose not to reveal his name, thus cutting himself off from further consideration the Lord would have been glad to show him, to let those present see how all-embracing his redemptive urge was. Instead, the spirit replied, "Legion, for there are many of us." This answer indicates that there were many in need of freeing.

States of possession like this give one a glimpse of something mysterious, incomprehensible, indeed horrifying: thousands of spirits looking for shelter in a human being or in subjection to a dark power that compels them to torment the living.

To return to our story, Gottliebin experienced another apparent instance of possession a few days later, though this time Blumhardt did not intervene as he had before. It seemed as if specific demons were now coming out of her by the hundreds. Every time it happened, the woman's face assumed a new, threatening mien. The demons, by their own admission, were not permitted to touch Blumhardt, but they did attack the others present, including the mayor, who received more than a few blows. Gottliebin meanwhile yanked her hair, beat her breasts, banged her head against the wall, and tried to injure herself in other ways, though a few simple words from Blumhardt seemed to calm her.

As these scenes grew increasingly terrible, Blumhardt's presence sometimes seemed to make matters worse. He related:

> No words can describe what I endured in soul and spirit at that time. I so badly wanted to have done with the matter. True, in each instance I could depart with inward satisfaction, believing that the demonic power had given way and that the tormented woman was again completely all right. However, the dark powers always seemed to gain fresh strength, so intent were they on entangling me in a labyrinth and ruining me.
>
> All my friends advised me to give up. But I thought with horror of what might become of Gottliebin if I withdrew my support, and how everyone would consider it my fault if things turned out badly. I would endanger myself and others if I tried to extricate myself by withdrawing. I felt caught in a net. I must also admit that I felt ashamed to give in

to the devil – in my own heart and before my Savior, whose active help I had experienced so many times. I often had to ask myself, "Who is Lord?" And I always heard an inner voice call: "Forward! We may first have to descend into the deepest depths, but it must come to a good end, if it is true that Jesus crushed the Serpent's head."

As the scenes in which demons came out of Gottliebin grew more frequent, there were other mysterious occurrences as well. For example, one night when she was asleep, Gottliebin felt a scorching hand grab her throat, leaving large burns behind. Her aunt, who slept in the same room, lit a lamp, and found blisters around Gottliebin's neck. Day and night Gottliebin would receive unexplainable blows to her head or side. On top of this invisible objects tripped her in the street or on the stairs, causing sudden falls and resulting in bruises and other injuries.

On June 25, 1842, Blumhardt was informed that Gottliebin had gone mad. When he called on her the following morning, everything seemed to be well. However, in the afternoon Gottliebin suffered such a violent attack that it left her as if dead. Once again it appeared that demons were coming out of her, with a force that exceeded anything Blumhardt had experienced previously. To him, it felt like a victory of incomprehensible magnitude. For the next several weeks nothing much happened, and Gottliebin walked the village unmolested and unharmed. "It was a time of rejoicing for me," Blumhardt later said.

He had earned that joy. Even his best friends had warned him not to get involved in the conflict. But Blumhardt had acted boldly, staking everything on his assurance that Jesus Christ is the same today as he was two thousand years ago, when for the sake of suffering humankind, he had stopped the powers of darkness in their tracks. He had remained at his post like a soldier, neither advancing rashly nor retreating, and had held the field.

When the fight was at its fiercest, on July 9, 1842, he wrote to his predecessor and mentor Barth, "Whenever I write the name of Jesus, I am overcome by a holy awe and by a joyous, fervent sense of gratitude that he is mine. Only now have I truly come to know what we have in him."

But if anyone thought the fight was now over, they were wrong. As Blumhardt put it, he seemed to have taken on an enemy who constantly brought out fresh troops.

In August 1842 Gottliebin came to him, pale and disfigured, to tell him something she had been too shy to reveal but could keep hidden no longer. At first she hedged, making him tense and apprehensive, but finally came out and told him how every Wednesday and Friday she would bleed so painfully and severely that she was sure she was dying. In her description of other things she experienced in connection with this bleeding, Blumhardt recognized several bizarre fantasies of popular superstition, apparently become reality. He later recalled:

> To begin with, I needed time to collect my thoughts, as I realized what a hold the power of darkness had gained over humanity. My next thought was "Now you are done for; now you are getting into magic and witchcraft, and what can you do to protect yourself against them?" But as I looked at her in her distress, I shuddered to think that such darkness could be possible, and help impossible. I recalled that there are people thought to have secret powers enabling them to ward off all manner of demonic evils; I thought of the sympathetic magic that people swear by. Should I look around for something of that sort? But I couldn't. I had already long felt that that would be using devils to drive out devils. At one point, it is true, I considered affixing the name of Jesus to the door of a sick person's house, but then I found a warning in Galatians 3:3: "Can it be that you are so stupid? You started with the spiritual; do you now look to the material?" I took this as a reminder to keep to the pure weapons of prayer and God's word.
>
> Questions flooded through me: Cannot the prayers of the faithful prevail against this satanic power, whatever it be? What are we poor people to do if we cannot call down direct help from above? Because Satan has a hand in it, must we leave it at

that? Can he not be defeated through faith? If Jesus came to destroy the works of the devil, ought we not to hold on to that? If magic and witchcraft are at work, is it not a sin to let them continue unchecked when they could be confronted?

With these thoughts I struggled through to faith in the power of prayer, where no other counsel was to be had. I said to Gottliebin, "We are going to pray; come what may, we shall dare it! There is nothing to lose. Almost every page of Scripture tells of prayer being heard. God will keep his promises." I let her go with the assurance that I would pray for her and asked her to keep me informed.

The next day, a Friday, was unforgettable. Toward evening – as the first storm clouds in months began to gather across the sky – Gottliebin was thrown into a veritable frenzy. First she raced madly from room to room looking for a knife so she could kill herself. Then, running up to the attic, she sprang onto a windowsill. While standing on the ledge, ready to jump, the first lightning of the approaching storm startled her and brought her to her senses. "For God's sake, I don't want that!" she cried. But her sanity lasted only a moment. Once more delirious, she took a rope – later she was not able to say how it had come into her hands – wound it artfully around a beam in the loft, and made a slip knot. Just as she pushed her head through the noose, a second flash of lightning caught her eye and brought her around as before. The next morning when she saw the noose on the beam, she wept, claiming that in a sober state of mind she never could have tied such a clever knot.

At eight o'clock the same evening, Blumhardt was called to Gottliebin and found her in a pool of blood. He said a few comforting words to her, but she did not respond. Then, as thunder rolled outside, he began to pray earnestly.

> As I prayed, the anger of the demons afflicting Gottliebin broke loose with full force, howling and lamenting, "Now the game is up. Everything has been betrayed. You have ruined us completely. The whole pack is falling apart. It is all over. There is nothing but confusion, and it is all your fault. With your unceasing praying you will drive us out completely. Alas, alas, everything is lost! We are 1,067, but there are many others still alive, and they ought to be warned! Oh, woe to them, they are lost! God forsworn – forever forlorn!"
>
> The howls of the demons, the flashes of lightning, the rolling thunder, the splashing of the downpour, the earnestness of all present, and my prayers, which seemed to literally draw the demons out – all this created a scene that is very difficult to imagine. Among other things, the demons yelled, "Nobody could have driven us out! Only you have managed it, you with your persistent praying."

After fifteen minutes of intercession, Gottliebin came to and Blumhardt and the others left the room while she changed her clothes. As he tells it, "When we came back and found her sitting on her bed, she was a completely different person. There was no room in us for anything but praise and thanks. The bleeding had ended for good."

Before long other demonic manifestations made their appearance. Blumhardt, unable to see the way forward, poured out his need to a friend, the director of a seminary, who pointed him to Jesus' words, "There is no means of casting out this sort but by prayer and fasting" (Matt. 17:21). Thinking on it further, Blumhardt began to wonder whether fasting might not be more meaningful than he had previously assumed:

> Insofar as fasting enhances the intensity of prayer and shows God the urgency of the person praying (in fact, it represents a continuous prayer without words), I believed it could prove effective, particularly since this was specific divine advice for the case at hand. I tried it, without telling anybody, and found it a tremendous help during the fight. It enabled me to be much calmer, firmer, and clearer in my speech. I no longer needed to be present for long stretches; I sensed that I could make my influence felt without even being there. And when I did come, I often noticed results within a few moments.

A few other accounts of demonic manifestations are worth mentioning here too. Blumhardt tells, for example, of apparent differences among the demons.

Some were defiant and full of hatred toward him, crying, among other things, "You are our worst enemy, and we are your enemies. Oh, if only we could do what we want!" Some expressed a horror of the abyss, which they perceived to be very near, and uttered things such as, "Would that there were no God in heaven!" And yet they assumed full responsibility for their own downfall. One particularly dreadful demon, whom Gottliebin had seen earlier in her house and who now admitted to being a perjurer, repeatedly exclaimed the words painted on the window shutter of that house:

> Man, think on eternity,
> And do not mock the time of grace,
> For judgment is not far off.

Then he would fall silent, contort his face, stiffly raise three of the sick woman's fingers, and then shudder and groan. There were many bizarre scenes of this kind, and Blumhardt would gladly have welcomed more witnesses to corroborate his reports of them.

In general, most of the demons that showed themselves in Möttlingen between August 1842 and December 1843 desperately yearned for liberation from the bonds of Satan. They used various languages to express themselves, including Italian, French, German, and other languages which Blumhardt could not recognize.

Now and then there were utterances that could not be assigned to any particular demon; they sounded as if they came from some other source. One voice repeated Habakkuk 2:3–4 numerous times: "There is still a vision for the appointed time. At the destined hour it will come in breathless haste, it will not fail. If it delays, wait for it; for when it comes will be no time to linger. The reckless will be unsure of himself, while the righteous will live by being faithful." The same voice also addressed the demons and recited a Bible passage Blumhardt later identified as Jeremiah 3:25: " You have sinned against the Lord your God, both you and your fathers, from your youth till now, and you have not obeyed the Lord your God." Blumhardt wrote:

> At first I did not grasp the importance of these ut-
> terances, but then I began to feel that they deserved
> greater attention. Listening to them I sensed that
> they came from above to strengthen and comfort
> me.

On occasion, Blumhardt responded to demons that longed to be set free:

> For a long time I would not listen to their talk. But I
> often found myself in a dilemma, seeing how they
> showed themselves in Gottliebin's tormented fea-
> tures, her hands raised in supplication, her streaming
> tears, and the sounds that came from her – sighs and
> groans of fear, despair, and entreaty that would melt
> a heart of stone. I resisted becoming involved in any

attempt at freeing them, because everything I had experienced made me suspect a pernicious ruse of the devil and made me fear for my reputation. But in the end I could not help at least trying, since those demons that appeared to have some hope for themselves could not be moved by threats or exhortations.

The first demon I attempted to help was that of the woman who seemed to have been at the root of the whole affair. Reappearing in Gottliebin, she declared in a firm and decisive voice that she wanted to belong to the Savior and not to the devil.

At this point the woman asked Blumhardt, "Who are you?" When he answered, "A servant of the gospel," she replied, "Yes, and what a hard one!" This response shook Blumhardt to the core. Then he asked her, "Where are you?" and she said, "In the chasm."

Then she told me how much had changed in the spirit world because of this fight, and that I had succeeded thus far only because I had relied solely on the word of God, and on prayer. If I had resorted to popular means of warding off evil spirits – remedies and spells and cures – I would have been trapped. The demon raised a finger to emphasize her point and ended with the words, "It is a dreadful battle that you have undertaken!" Then she pleaded with me to pray for her to be released from the devil's power – she had unwittingly fallen into his thrall by dabbling in idolatry, sorcery, and sympathetic magic – and to be given a place of rest. I had known this woman well in her lifetime; she had shown a hunger for the word of God such as I had rarely seen. My heart ached for her. Glancing toward heaven, I asked her, "But where do you want to go?"

"I should like to remain in your house," she said. Taken aback, I said, "That cannot be."

"May I go into the church?"

I considered this request a moment and then replied, "If you promise not to disturb anybody and never make yourself visible, I would have no objection – if Jesus permits it."

This was risky, perhaps, but I trusted that God would set everything right, and felt no presumption before him. The spirit seemed satisfied, named the farthest corner as the place where she would be, and then seemed to come out of Gottliebin willingly and easily. No one told Gottliebin any of this, though to her horror she later saw the woman at the designated place in the church. Apart from her, however, nobody noticed anything, and the spirit soon vanished for good.

There were subsequent struggles with other spirits who also claimed to love God but were still bound to the devil through idolatry and sorcery. They, too, sought liberation and security. Only with utmost caution and after consulting the Lord did I consent to their requests. My standard reply was, "If Jesus permits it."

It soon became evident that there was indeed divine guidance in all this, for not all were granted what they asked for. Some had to depart relying only on God's mercy. I do not wish to expound on this beyond saying that it always brought relief to Gottliebin. One interesting case I cannot leave unmentioned, however. To one of the spirits who asked to be let into the church, I answered as usual, "If Jesus permits it." After a while he burst out crying desperately, saying, "God is a judge for widows and orphans!" and declaring that he had not been permitted to enter the church.

I replied, "You see, it is the Lord who shows you the way; what I say doesn't count. Go where the Lord bids you go."

He continued, "May I go into your house?"

I was again startled by this request and, thinking of my wife and children, was not inclined to accede to it. Then it occurred to me that this might be a test to see if I was really ready for any sacrifice, so I said, "If you do not disturb anybody, and if Jesus permits it, it would be all right." At this a voice cried from within Gottliebin, "Not under any roof! God is a judge for widows and orphans!" Once more the spirit seemed to burst into tears and asked if he might at least go into my garden. That request was granted. Apparently, the demon was guilty of having made orphans homeless.

Blumhardt's experiences contradict the assumption that after death we immediately find ourselves either eternally blessed or eternally damned, and that there are only two places for the dead: heaven or hell. Still, he rejected the notion of a purgatory – a stage of the afterlife where souls are purified by torment – and he refuted the charge that he tried to convert spirits:

> For me, it was never a question of conversion, but rather of freeing the souls of otherwise believing persons. These had been involved in magical practices, which during their lifetime they had not recognized as sins. Because of this they had remained under the devil's control without knowing it. Since even in these sins they had not meant to turn away from God, they were in need not of conversion but merely of liberation. They could only find such liberation, however, if somewhere on earth a battle was being waged, in firm faith in the blood of Jesus Christ, against the power of magic.

In this regard, a passage in Paul's letter to the Romans was of utmost importance to Blumhardt:

> The created universe waits with eager expectation for God's sons to be revealed. It was made the victim of frustration, not by its own choice, but because of him who made it so; yet always there was hope, because the universe itself is to be freed from the shackles of mortality and enter into the liberty and splendor of the children of God. Up to the present, we know, the whole created universe groans in all its parts as if in pangs of childbirth. Not only so, but even we, to whom the Spirit is given as firstfruits of the harvest to

come, are groaning inwardly while we wait for God to make us his sons and set our whole body free (Rom. 8:19–23).

If so much forgiveness is reserved for the last judgment, might not the yearning of "the created universe" be related to this? Yet people take the liberty to exclude from the universe all those who die unredeemed. As Blumhardt once commented:

Nobody thinks of the dead, and yet there are billions of them. Their guilt is often not very great if one considers that most of them are pagans not responsible for their ignorance. Seen in that light, the statement that the world is in bondage to evil takes on much deeper meaning. The apostle's thought that the whole universe has fallen prey to this power of lying and death is as shattering as the other thought is uplifting: that through Christ's ultimate victory, creation will be liberated from this bondage.

During his fight Blumhardt began to see the importance of Jesus' promise, "Whatever you ask in my name, I will do." It became clear to him that the coming of God cannot merely be expected passively, but must be prepared through victories of faith won by the church:

I can hardly believe that the Lord will simply turn up one fine day and slay the devil without the faithful having to be greatly concerned about it. Then, when these events threatened to continue indefinitely, I rallied all my inner strength and begged God that he, the power who made everything out of nothing, might now reduce these things to nothingness and utterly undo the devil's trickery. In this way I struggled for several days, and the Lord – who promised "Whatever you will ask in my name, I will do" – kept his word!

Of course, most people take a completely different attitude regarding the kingdom of darkness and its impact on humanity. In general, people are careful not to say what they think about it. They even consider it the first duty of an enlightened mind to deny the existence of Satan's realm. When confronted by otherwise inexplicable facts, they prefer to turn off the machinery of their intellect. True, it may be better to dismiss such phenomena as Blumhardt witnessed in Gottliebin than to indulge in undue curiosity and exploration. In fact, his aversion to inquisitive dabbling gave him the objectivity and resolve he needed for a fight of such demonic dimensions.

Several times during Blumhardt's struggle there was a surcease, but following such periods the forces of darkness assailed Gottliebin with renewed vigor, as if determined to kill her. On one occasion, after she had wounded herself dreadfully and the wounds had healed, they suddenly burst open again. A friend hurried to Blumhardt with the message that every minute's delay would be perilous. Blumhardt recalled:

At that I fell on my knees in my room and in my distress spoke bold words. This time – my faith had become so strong – I decided I was not even going to do the devil the honor of going to Gottliebin's house. Rather, I sent a message back with Gottliebin's friend asking her to get up and come to me, adding that with faith she would have strength to do it. Before long, there she was, coming up the stairs. No one can possibly know how that made me feel.

Around Christmas 1843, from December 24 to 28, the fight finally came to a climactic and decisive conclusion. In Blumhardt's own words:

It seemed as if all the evil powers that had appeared before were joining forces for a combined assault. Most disconcerting was that now these sinister workings affected Gottliebin's brother Hans and her sister Katharina, so that I had to fight a most desperate battle for all three of them at once. I can no longer tell the exact order of events; so many things happened that I cannot possibly recall them all, but those were days I never want to experience again. It had come to the point where I simply had to risk everything; it was a question of victory or death. Great as my own efforts were, I sensed a tangible divine protection. I did not feel the least bit tired or worn out, even after forty hours of watching, fasting, and praying.

Gottliebin's brother was the first to regain freedom from his apparent posession – so much so that he could aid me in what followed. This time the brunt of the attack was not directed at Gottliebin, who seemed to be completely at peace, but at her sister Katharina, who up till then had not been affected at all. Katharina now began to rage so furiously that it took great efforts to control her. She threatened to break me into a thousand pieces, and I did not risk going near her. She also made continuous attempts to injure herself and slyly looked around for opportunities to injure those holding her as well. At the same time she kept babbling and ranting so horribly that thousands of spiteful tongues seemed to be speaking all at once.

Remarkably, Katharina remained fully conscious, and one could reason with her. When admonished, she would say she could not control her speech and behavior, and asked us to keep a firm hold on her to prevent her from doing something terrible. Afterward, too, she remembered everything distinctly, which depressed her so severely that I had to spend days counseling and encouraging her. Gradually, after much prayer, these memories faded away.

The demon inside Katharina did not make himself out to be a departed human spirit, but an eminent angel of Satan. He claimed that if he were forced to descend into the abyss, it would deal Satan a fatal blow, but would also cause Katharina to bleed to death. All of a sudden, at midnight, a series of desperate howls issued from Katharina's throat. Lasting for about a quarter of an hour, the cries were gruesomely forceful, and so loud that half the inhabitants of the village heard them. At the same time Katharina started shaking so violently that it seemed her limbs would come loose. The demonic voice expressed fear and despair mingled with tremendous arrogance and defiance. It demanded that God perform a sign to allow it to go to hell with at least some honor, instead of forcing it to abdicate like an ordinary sinner.

Then, at two o'clock in the morning, while Katharina arched her upper body backward over her chair, the purported angel of Satan, in a voice no human throat could make, bellowed out the words, "Jesus is the victor! Jesus is the victor!" Everyone in the village who heard these words understood their significance, and they left an indelible impression on many. The strength and power of the demon now appeared to wane with every passing minute. It grew quieter, moved less and less, and finally left Katharina altogether unnoticed – just as the light of life goes out in a dying person – around eight o'clock in the morning.

At this point the two-year-long fight came to an end. True, there remained things to work through afterward, but that was like clearing away the rubble of a collapsed building. Hans, for instance, was subject to a few more attacks, but they were scarcely noticed by others. Katharina had occasional convulsions as well, but soon she, too, recovered fully. Further incidents were insignificant and unnoticed by others.

As for Gottliebin, she suffered from several renewed attempts on the part of the dark power during the following months, but these attacks were doomed to failure and did not claim much of my attention. Eventually she attained complete health. All her former ailments, well known to her physicians, completely disappeared – the high shoulder, the short leg, stomach troubles, and others. Over a considerable time her health has remained stable in every respect, which is a miracle of God.

Gottliebin's disposition, too, has improved in a most gratifying way; her humility, her sincere and sensible way of speaking, coupled with decisiveness and modesty, have helped many others. I know of no other woman who can handle children with such insight, love, and patience. I often entrust my own children to her. During the past year she has taught handicrafts; now I am starting a nursery school, and have not been able to find anyone as suitable as she to direct it.

In 1850 Blumhardt commented on Gottliebin's subsequent life and work:

Since she became part of my household, Gottliebin has been my wife's most loyal and sensible support in managing the household and raising the children. Others can testify to her faithfulness in this role, and her effect on those who pass through the house. Everyone who knows her speaks of her with respect and appreciation. She has become nearly indispensable to me, particularly in the treatment of mentally ill people, who usually develop such a trust in her that they require little of my time. She is not

employed by us as a domestic servant, for her gratitude will not allow her to accept payment for her
work. Rather, she considers herself one of the family, as do her sister Katharina and her brother Hans.

Hans became the handyman in Blumhardt's rectory,
as adept at splitting wood as at dealing with mentally ill persons, for which he, too, had a special tal-
ent. Blumhardt fondly called him his majordomo.

Thus the fight, which had for a time threatened to
take on increasingly bizarre dimensions, ended for
good. One consequence of the conflict was that
Blumhardt found himself increasingly isolated.
Friends all but abandoned him, and even his confi-
dant, Barth, no longer seemed to understand him, as
the following letter from Blumhardt indicates.

Written to Barth on January 2, 1844, it should not
be misconstrued as proof of a deteriorating relationship between the two men. Certainly Blumhardt
complains that Barth had been overbearing, but
their relationship had always been marked by honesty and blunt speaking, and they remained lifelong
friends:

You wanted to dictate to me, but had I followed you,
I surely would have been undone. You ought to
know that he who turns his back on the opponent is
lost. You yourself said that the Enemy's aim was to
ruin me. That is true, but for the sake of Christ I ask
you to tell me openly: is there no power in the world
other than that of the devil? Are you suggesting that

I should have handled him with kid gloves like a devil-worshipper, letting him do as he pleases, to keep him from assaulting me? Open your eyes, my dear brother, and tell me: Doesn't the devil seek everyone's ruin? And don't you agree that I would be in greater danger of being ruined if I withdrew into a snail shell instead of confronting the devil head-on with the word of God? O brother, you do not seem to know the unspeakable distress weighing on poor humankind!

You do not know or do not bear in mind the full, horrible extent of magical practices and alliances with the devil in Christendom and in the world at large. But to come to know this, to be quite certain of it, and then to back out – why, that would make me worse than the devil! Well, know that I dared it. I wanted to see if Jesus could break the devil's neck. I felt driven to do it, as you know. I wanted to see who would tire and throw in the towel first – the devil or I. I dared it; I fought. Guided by God's word day by day, for a whole year and a half, my cries to God could not possibly go unanswered. That I am right in this belief will surely be confirmed on that great day, when Jesus, who has been merciful to me, will vindicate me.

In fact, he has already vindicated me. You ought to see how happy I am after each bout – like a child – and how full of gratitude. And how I have learned to pray, so that there are many things I need only ask of the Savior and I receive them. This is especially noticeable in regard to the children, and my dear wife Doris simply brims over with joy because of it. One sigh to him above, "Lord, give me strength!" is enough to restore me. Even after the hardest night-long struggles, I am sure no one can tell by my face what I have been through. Ask anyone if they thought me worn-out or weakened this week, during which I stood fifteen times before my congregation and went without sleep for forty hours straight.

After reading Blumhardt's graphic description of his fight against the kingdom of darkness, it is well to remember his warning that we can withstand this darkness only to the degree that we experience the light of Jesus, the Redeemer. True, an awareness of Jesus' presence during the fight in Möttlingen was often overshadowed by the more dramatic appearance of evil powers. But it is clear which forces were victorious. In any case, the most incredible and dramatic chapter of the story was still to come.

III   THE AWAKENING

Blumhardt's fight came to an end on December 28, 1843, but with the close of that chapter came the opening of a new, even more significant one: a widespread movement of repentance and renewal that changed hundreds of lives and spread far beyond the town.

Because of its raw drama, Blumhardt's fight for Gottliebin's soul tended to interest his contemporaries more than the awakening that followed. This pained Blumhardt. When an old friend begged him for a copy of *An Account of Gottliebin Dittus' Illness,* he handed it over only after some hesitation, reminding him, "But you know, this is not Möttlingen!" To Blumhardt, Möttlingen's significance lay in the change it experienced after the fight, not in the notoriety it gained because of the fight itself.

Blumhardt's fight had engendered a sober mood in his congregation, but its impact was greatest on him, his family, and his two closest supporters, the Mayor Kraushaar and Mose Stanger. For them, as well as for Gottliebin, it was a time of judgment and repentance. Insights kept coming to them from the Bible, and the new awareness they brought was piercing and punishing. "We were being curried with an iron comb," one of them said.

Already before the fight in 1841, the first harbinger of the awakening showed itself – in Blumhardt's confirmation classes. He told of one striking incident:

> With my twenty or so pupils sitting around me, I noticed that one of the boys – a troublemaker whom some had written off as a lost cause – was crying. Tears were streaming down his face. I didn't know what to make of it, so I had him stay behind after class and asked, "What's the matter with you? Why are you crying?" Trustingly, he told me he had heard a voice whisper in his ear, "Your sins are forgiven." I never expected anything like that and cannot recall any similar occurrence. From then on, the boy was a completely different person.

Then, on Good Friday 1842, just before the beginning of the fight, Blumhardt sensed another breakthrough. At the time church attendance was fair at Möttlingen, even at the notoriously independent parish branch of Haugstett. But everyone slept in church.

Blumhardt tended to be lenient with people who couldn't keep their eyes open while he preached. If hard work, sleeplessness, or sickness was to blame, he would likely tell them, "Have a little snooze then! It will do you good, and afterward you can be more attentive." But he also said, "Some of them are sleeping simply because they are satisfied with who they are. They think they know everything, and if they hear anything new, it only annoys them. They are not ready for a new burst of life. And what can you say in cases like that? You just have to let them sleep."

But this Good Friday, sitting in the sacristy before the service, Blumhardt couldn't bear the thought of watching his congregation snooze on such a holy day. Desperate, he cried to God from the depths of his heart, and felt he was heard. Then he went out, fortified, scrapped his prepared sermon and preached instead on John 19:26–27: "Woman, behold, your son… Behold, your mother!" According to those who were there, Blumhardt spoke so passionately about the Savior's love of his own that the drooping heads popped up one by one in surprise; people began to listen and, captivated, went on listening. The sleepiness was gone, never to return.

The real awakening, however, started around Christmas 1843, on that last decisive night of the fight when so many heard the cry, "Jesus is the victor!" The following morning others up and down the valley reported hearing, at the same hour, mournful cries of, "Into the abyss! Into the abyss!" Everybody was disquieted. Blumhardt reported: "They don't talk much about it in the village; but there is obvious amazement and trembling. One after another, they are coming to me and confessing their sins." Again, it was among members of his confirmation class that he first noticed a new movement afoot. He received letters from several of them secretly confessing their sins. In his classes, the change was tangible. Without telling him, some of the boys even began meeting in one or the other house to pray.

As 1844 began, the movement spread to the adults in the parish. On New Year's Eve a young Möttlingen man known for his revelry and his temper showed up at the rectory entrance. He had, in Blumhardt's opinion, "a bad reputation and a nature so twisted that I avoided talking to him, for fear of being lied to." Now this man stood shamefaced at the door, and asked Hans if he could see the pastor.

"What do you want to see the pastor for?" asked a skeptical Hans.

"Oh, Hans," he replied, "I am miserable! Last night I was in hell. I was told there that the only way to get out again was to see the pastor."

Hans took him upstairs to the Blumhardt's study. Blumhardt offered him a chair, but he said, "No, pastor, I belong on the sinner's bench." Hans, realizing that the man was in bitter earnest, left the room. Blumhardt remembered:

> Pale and trembling and not at all himself, he asked me, "Pastor, do you think I can still find forgiveness and salvation?" He claimed he had not been able to sleep for a whole week. If he could not get his burdens off his chest, he said, it would kill him. I remained somewhat reserved and told him straight out that until he confessed his sins in specific, I could not trust his sincerity. But I could not bring myself to let such a distraught man go without

praying with him. Doing something I had never done before, I laid my hands on him and said a few words of blessing, which visibly comforted him.

Two days later the man returned. Blumhardt wrote to Barth, "Yesterday the poor sinner was back, looking so brokenhearted and distressed as he stood in the doorway that the sight of him made one of the housemaids weep." This time the man intended to confess his sins, but still could not bring himself to do so. On his third visit he finally declared, "Now I am going to confess." – and did.

> He confessed his sins, with remarkable honesty, and it gave me my first real insight into the many evils rampant among our people. He was still greatly troubled, and my comfort had no lasting effect. He said that to give him complete peace, I would have to pronounce forgiveness in the authority of my office; he wanted to have his sins formally forgiven. Since I saw no reason not to fulfill his request, I laid my hands on his head and declared that his sins were forgiven. When he rose from his knees, his face radiated with gratitude.

This was the second turning point in Blumhardt's life. The first – the response to his cry, "Lord Jesus, help!" – had led him into grim conflicts and only through them to a memorable victory. This time the reward fell into his lap unexpectedly. Blumhardt later wrote about this important moment:

I can never forget the impression that the absolution made on that man and on me. An unspeakable joy shone from his face. I felt drawn into a completely new sphere, in which holy spiritual powers were at work. I could not yet understand it, nor did I try to, but I continued to act in the same simple and cautious way when others came along.

As the visitor left the rectory, he cheerfully told Hans, "Now I must go back and to talk to my friends. They've listened to my dirty jokes; now they can listen when I tell them how they can find salvation." And he kept his word. The next day he was back at the rectory, bringing along another man, just as remorseful as he had been. Same procedure, same result. Soon another came, and another.

A few weeks later Blumhardt was reporting that an influx of people wanting to confess kept him constantly busy "from seven o'clock in the morning until eleven o'clock at night. Some whom I never would have expected sat in the living room for hours, silent and withdrawn as they waited their turn."

On January 27 Blumhardt wrote to Barth:

People kept coming until eight o'clock in the evening. Already sixteen people have made their confessions to me. With ten of them I am finished for the present, though I generally hold off with offering absolution. Everybody has to come at least three times, and several who did not find peace because they were still hiding something came six or eight times. Another thing: One of the town drunks has not touched a drink since last Monday. I heard it from him and from his wife yesterday morning.

Three days later he wrote again:

Yesterday, from eight in the morning until eleven at night, there was one caller after another, a total of thirty-five, all suffering severe pangs of conscience and looking for peace. Some wept so bitterly in their distress that I granted absolution the first time they came, for their hearts seemed about to burst. In all, twenty-four have found peace. These newly awakened men and women gather every evening in various houses.

By early February Blumhardt reported that the total number of visitors coming to confess to him had reached sixty-seven. Blumhardt's manner toward his callers was gentle, more passive than pressing, but he insisted on the truth and rejected any excuses.

When I ask some people what makes them come, they say they have watched others become happy and wanted the same. Certainly, much is still lacking in these people, yet having come once, they are inevitably drawn in. How everything is changing! In every house, people are gathering and turning to God. May he help me to combine prudence and wisdom with patience and love.

The movement reached Haugstett as well. Some who mocked it at first or chided their wives for going turned up themselves a week later, shedding tears of remorse for their hostile attitude and confessing that they had found no rest or peace since.

It took some time for the prayer meeting attendees – the real pietists – to show up. In the rectory yard one evening, one of their leaders came up to Hans and said, "You know, what Pastor Blumhardt is doing now is really Catholic stuff!"

"You think so?" replied Hans, "He doesn't ask people to confess. But when they come seeking peace, he serves them as every pastor should. Have you found forgiveness for your sins?"

"Yes."

"Well, then let others find it too."

A few days later the man was back. He first apologized to Hans for his criticism, which he said had weighed heavily on his conscience ever since. Then, like the others, he went to see Blumhardt and returned, no longer a self-righteous saint but a contrite sinner.

Another member of the prayer meeting, a man highly respected for his devout, honorable character, called at the rectory. Meeting Blumhardt on the stairs, he said, "Pastor Blumhardt, I thought that since everybody else is coming to see you, I…"

"Is something bothering you, too?" Blumhardt interrupted.

"Well, not exactly," the man replied.

"Of course not. You are the dear, good Mr. A.," Blumhardt said warmly, shook his hand, and excusing himself, bade him farewell. Early the next morning there was Mr. A., waiting to speak to Blumhardt. He had had a terrible night, in which he had been made aware of all his sins; and now he was back, not as the good and respectable Mr. A. but as one of many sinners. Later Blumhardt commented, "I thought he would come; I had him in my prayers the whole time."

Blumhardt's work kept growing. In a letter written on February 10, he said:

Every day I have people with me until half past eleven at night. The next morning at six somebody is already waiting, and this goes on without a letup all day long. I can hardly think of anything else. At the children's service yesterday, I asked to be excused from talks because of my work for the monthly newspaper. As a result I can expect even more callers today...What am I to do about it all? It has gone beyond anything I can imagine. By now 156 people have come, shedding tears of repentance, if not the first time, then the second or third time. How I can handle it is a mystery to me. If only you knew the many sins I hear about, which often make me freeze with horror, you would be able to understand the difficulties of my position...The various gatherings are getting so crowded I shall soon have to do some organizing.

A week later, the number of repentant visitors had risen to 222. In a letter Barth wrote to a friend around this time, he recalls:

> I was recently in Möttlingen and met several of those newly awakened; it was a pleasure to see them. True, among them are some who had already been members of the prayer meeting for a long time, but even they had not been single-minded. Now they have been gripped afresh by the new life. In my eyes the whole thing is a miracle.

Later Barth wrote again:

> For years we go on scattering the seed – we know it is good seed, and that the seed merchant has not cheated us – yet nothing will come up, and people stay exactly the same. Still, nothing is really lost; it just takes a long time for some things to germinate. Möttlingen is the perfect example of this. Machtolf preached ardently for thirty-seven years, after him, Gross preached for fourteen more. I continued tilling the same old ground there for another fourteen years, hoping at least for some small harvest from the sowing of my predecessors. But that was not granted, nor did I deserve it.
>
> Then my successor Blumhardt took the pulpit. For the first five years, things only seemed to grow worse. Moral standards declined and the spiritual life of the parish ebbed away. But now a fire has started, and it continues to spread. One person after another has been seeking out the minister. The toughest and

wildest have come, dejectedly weeping, but then, after confessing their sins, they are full of the peace of forgiveness. Frightful secret sins have come to light – sins which are likely widespread. By now over 350 people have come, from eighty-year-olds down to schoolchildren, and the conflagration even has spread to the parish branch in Haugstett, which until recently appeared absolutely unreceptive. More than twenty people have come from there.

People constantly speak of the insights they had received from Machtolf, Gross, and myself, which they long tried to suppress but which they are now trying to act on. In particular, the importance of our confirmation classes has become clear, for nearly all admit to having had their consciences pricked then.

————

As weeks turned to months, the awakening went on and Blumhardt continued to keep his friend informed. In early March he wrote:

> Imagine! Yesterday I heard that all twenty-four members of my confirmation class have been meeting daily on their own. They sing, read from the Bible, and pray on their knees, with everyone taking a turn. The one most inspired leads the meeting and questions the others about what they have read.

Everything is done in such a childlike and innocent way that one cannot listen without being deeply moved.

But even if Blumhardt was grateful for this movement of heart, he was not one to sit back and gloat. On the contrary, he felt that what he was experiencing was just a foretaste of a larger divine plan, and he yearned that others might take part in it. "I long for another outpouring of the Holy Spirit, another Pentecost. That must come if things are to change in Christianity, for it simply cannot continue in such a wretched state. The gifts and powers of the early Christian time – oh, how I long for their return! And I believe the Savior is just waiting for us to ask for them."

This became the watchword of his life: Hope and pray for a new outpouring of the Holy Spirit! Blumhardt never doubted that this spirit was constantly at work in the church, but he took issue when individual Christians claimed to possess it:

Is it really true that we have God's spirit? The Holy Spirit is supposed to be one, yet how many thousands of spirits, all priding themselves on being the spirit of truth, rule in Christendom! Who then has the Holy Spirit? The churches? But which of the innumerable shades among them, all at loggerheads with each other? I cannot understand how one can say that the Holy Spirit is present without being able to say where it is. ·

Much is known about the spirit of contention and wanting to be in the right – where one thinks one has the spirit of truth and others do not have it. But where is the other, the Comforter, the personal representative of God and Christ, who is to remain with those who have Christ…When I look at what we have, I cannot help sighing, "O Lord Jesus, is that the promised spirit for which you hung on a tree?" Where is the spirit that penetrates nation after nation as swiftly as at the time of the apostles and places them at Jesus' feet? And when we open our mouth to proclaim the gospel, where is the spirit that shakes people so deeply that they cry out, "What shall we do to be saved?"

The Holy Spirit must be tangible, even visible, as coming personally from God. It must drive out the forces of darkness from humankind, raise the disfigured human race to something better, and restrain all evil, even in the most corrupt people. That is how the Holy Spirit once showed itself, even if it does not seem to show itself now. If people want to close their eyes and think that the Holy Spirit is here, we have to let them talk. But they should kindly allow me to think differently.

If one imagines the long days Blumhardt spent in his study, and how much of what he heard there cut to his heart and demanded spiritual discernment, one realizes that his joy was often tempered by anguished soul-searching and stress. He wrote to Barth:

Unless I close the door, I do not have a moment to myself. And so far, I have not been able to do so, for people are often so tormented that they cannot wait. Yesterday one man was sent up long before his turn; the other visitors had told him, "You are hurting the most; you had better go up first." Yesterday I also had a conference with twenty men. (There will be even more today.) It lasted three hours, and by the end we all felt we had drawn much closer together...

In general, these conferences have made splendid progress – on Monday thirty-one adolescent boys, Tuesday twenty-one men, Wednesday forty-six men. All of them spoke sincerely and warmly. On Thursday thirty-three women came, and yesterday fifty others. Everything went very well.

In early March Blumhardt wrote:

Yesterday morning I had personal talks and worked on the monthly newspaper, and so got to Haugstett a little late. There I held a prayer meeting and a confirmation class, had talks with twenty-one adults, met with twenty-six children, and arrived home around six. Here people were already waiting. It was half past eleven before I got to the paper...Then, at two in the morning the doorbell rang: an old woman lay dying. I hurried to her and was able to comfort her somewhat, so I returned home, but I had scarcely arrived when the bell rang again: the mayor's child was dying! Off I set again, only to find the child dead when I arrived.

Blumhardt rejoiced in the way the children of the parish took part in the awakening, especially their habit of meeting on their own to pray. But he opposed all affectations of piety. When told, for instance, that schoolchildren were meeting for prayer during their free time but then drifting into class late and absent-minded because of it, he said, "I would have boxed their ears if I were the teacher! What is the use of such prayer?" Still, Blumhardt was relieved by the disappearance of the "brooding" he had sensed among the village children, and refreshed by those who came to his study to receive his blessing – and, in some cases, to confess wrongdoings.

In mid-March Blumhardt wrote to Barth:

There have been many joys and struggles side by side, as it should be. No matter – every day is a day of victory, for I say, "The more fights, the more victories!" I am not one for giving in, and I am confident that everything will turn out well.

By Easter, with very few exceptions, the movement had taken hold of the entire congregation, including Haugstett. During the winter it had also spread to neighboring villages, and to some extent, even farther into the Black Forest. As fast as it was discussed – and ridiculed – it spread further. Naturally, the awakening made some of the scoffers curious, and before long they were coming, too. Crowds from other parishes began to attend his Sunday services too and even special services such as weddings and funerals. Once, arriving for the funeral of some little-known person, Blumhardt was astonished to find his church full of strangers. On April 6 he wrote to Barth, "The churchyard can no longer contain all the listeners."

Far from being pleased with himself when members of other congregations showed up, Blumhardt was troubled, for he knew that the influx meant diminished attendance in other parishes. Writing in a church periodical, he worried:

What am I to do? How am I to channel the flood? This whole unusual movement has got me thinking. As it is taking place within the church, it should not be presumptuous to think that the Lord has a hand in it. If it is the Lord I am dealing with, rather than resist him with human considerations, I had better take upon myself whatever labor, sweat, worry, fear, misunderstandings, and conflict it might entail.

I have taken pains not to do anything designed to draw people, and nobody can say I flatter my visitors. In fact, I know of ministers who have encouraged their parishioners to go to Möttlingen. (Whether their visits have done them any good I leave for others to say.) But I am confident that before long my fellow ministers will have fuller churches than ever, and then the number of people flocking here will taper off of its own accord.

The private visits of outsiders to my home are even more burdensome. To be sure, I send those

whom I can back to their own pastors, and several
of these have thanked me for that. But some of my
colleagues do not share my belief in the value of private confession, and that makes things very awk-
ward. After all, some of their parishioners are so
weighed down by their sin they can hardly carry it
anymore.

I advise people – that is, those who do not find a
receptive ear in their pastor – to open their hearts
to a sincere and devoted friend, with prayer and in
the presence of God, according to the words of the
apostle James, "Confess your sins to one another." If
they repent deeply and long for complete inner renewal, they can be assured of forgiveness.

Occasionally a visitor shares with me some incident from his life that might appear to be a confession, but I must definitely refute rumors that I treat
outsiders like members of my own congregation,
thus encroaching on someone else's sphere of authority. I have never offered them absolution. But I
cannot say it emphatically enough: it would do to
my esteemed colleagues a world of good if they
would make their parishioner aware of their hidden
sins, and then offer them a chance to unburden
themselves.

It is hard to picture the earnestness with which this
movement took hold of some people, despite the inevitable mockery that accompanied it. If a villager
was known to be walking toward Möttlingen to see
Blumhardt, he was likely to be teased as a "pilgrim to

Möttlingen," or be laughed at: "Headed for Jerusalem? Have fun!"

Amazingly, the extravagant emotionalism often associated with so-called revivals was completely absent in Möttlingen. Nor were there the public avowals of repentance and declarations of wickedness. This awakening was much too serious for that, too deeply rooted in reality. People were driven by an inner compulsion.

Everywhere, guilty consciences were struck. Old enemies became reconciled. In several cases stolen goods were returned. In one shop, a well-dressed man rushed inside, put a coin on the counter, and rushed out again.

Not all efforts to set old wrongs right went smoothly. For example, a poor newlywed couple had barely managed to pay interest on a debt, when their creditor accidentally signed for two annual interest payments instead of one. The couple noticed the mistake when they got home and accepted it gratefully – as divine help, so to speak. Years passed. Now, caught up in the current of repentance, the couple confided the matter to Blumhardt and, following his advice, confessed the error to their creditor, asking for leniency and patience, since they were in no position to pay off the old debt. Unfortunately, the creditor responded with indignation and insisted on immediate payment.

Years later, in speaking of the motives that drive people to repent, Blumhardt shared his hopes for a movement encompassing all humankind:

A time will come when everybody will realize that they do not have what they ought to have. They will feel a painful emptiness and crave for something they don't even know. All of a sudden it will hit them: "How poor and weak we are, how miserable and depraved! How little certainty we have in what we think, believe, and hope!" Then they will look to those who appear to have what they lack.

That is how conversion begins. When the time is ripe, it will one day spread through the whole world. Then those who have what is right and true will be inundated by a flood of people yearning to have it, too. Oh, that this time might come soon!

One thing I have found to be vital in repenting is readiness to seek – and accept – help from others. The present genteel, self-loving brand of piety assumes, "I don't need anybody; I can set things right with God myself." But as long as people quietly try to work out their own salvation, they won't get anywhere. Only when they recognize the need for one another, and reach out and open up to one another will they move forward.

In a letter written in 1846 to a friend who had offered his impressions of the movement in Möttlingen, Blumhardt probed more deeply into the cause of the awakening and its relationship to the fight. This friend had suggested that the people, still in a state of shock, were primarily motivated by fear aroused by the terror of the fight. Blumhardt replied:

> I appreciate your remarks about life in Möttlingen. But it is a mistake to interpret the shock you write of as a mechanical response to frightening occurrences. The relationship between the fight and the awakening is not such an outward one. If anything, the awakening was a fruit of the fight, won by it. Through battle and victory, satanic powers were broken. They can no longer work at all, or can work only feebly. Spells that darkened hearts and minds were removed; minds formerly dull and closed became responsive. But since in their blindness people carelessly committed many outrageous deeds, it was only natural that their first reaction to the light should be one of shock at their true condition. In many cases they had never recognized their behavior as wrong, and suddenly it hit them so powerfully that they could no longer hide it from themselves.

An overview of the whole movement brings out its objectivity or, one might say, the imprint of its divine origin. There was nothing fabricated about it, either in Blumhardt or the people who came to him. They simply acted out of compunction. Blumhardt never so much as dreamed of such a movement, much less attempted to produce it.

To be sure, while embroiled in the fight he had been made aware that the power of sin lies in secrecy, and that most burdens are not lifted from a conscience until they are brought to light. And he had, in his hearty and brotherly way, begun to tell his Sunday listeners that if they had something on their consciences that robbed them of inner peace, they should come to him. As it was, he hardly needed to invite them to come to him, for he assumed they were in a repentant frame of mind. During the awakening it seemed his preaching itself uncovered the wrongs burdening his listeners, by casting a searching light into the innermost recesses of their hearts.

Blumhardt never attacked people with high-powered rhetoric to get them to repent. He disapproved of "converted" people assailing the "unconverted" or – following the motto, "strike while the iron is hot!" – using arguments or other persuasive tactics. It scared him to see sinners thrusting themselves upon other sinners, displaying their own supposedly new and admirable personalities, and warned that it would bear nothing but bad fruit, even when it might appear to result in conversions. "When will all these 'conversions' that leave heart and behavior unchanged come to an end?" he lamented.

Though some criticized Blumhardt for his forthright manners, others felt he was too gentle. Once when Blumhardt was invited to preach in another town, and the host minister complained afterward that he had spoken too kindly. Blumhardt replied,

"Everything in the gospel works toward repentance. Whatever flows from your own repentance works more repentance, but whatever does not spring from your own repentance is as effective as soap bubbles against fortress walls."

Blumhardt worried that many Christians show more concern about others' conversion than about their own: He said, "No matter how much gossip I may hear about the sins of another, they are none of my business until they are brought to me along with a plea for forgiveness. I know them only in the light of redemption. My task is never to judge, only to forgive. Christ came to save the world, not to judge it." Thus he carefully guarded the freedom of every individual. Privately, within his study, he would request the whole truth, but he was never pushy. When asked how much one ought to confess, he would advise, "Tell that which you would rather not tell." He was sometimes reluctant to offer absolution, not because a sin was too great or guilt too heavy, but because he wanted to be sure the person was not holding anything back.

Though Blumhardt disregarded his own person, he was not self-effacing but considered himself a servant called to act in the name of his Lord. Such strength and peace radiated from him that he was said to make one feel that Jesus Christ himself had stretched out his hand to the sinners who came to him. Several were reminded of the words, "Whatever you loose on earth shall be loosed in heaven," and, "If you forgive the sins of any, they are forgiven." This was one of the distinctive features of the awakening. But there were visible effects, too, as Blumhardt himself never tired of pointing out: "Many of the repentant feel a new strength flow through them, which has a physically healing effect. It rejuvenates their whole appearance."

In a letter to Barth, Blumhardt wrote of one Möttlingen man who, after climbing the stairs from the living room to the study and receiving Blumhardt's blessing, was so overcome by the certainty of forgiveness that he fell on the pastor's neck and smothered him with kisses. This forgiveness was such a source of redemption and liberation that people did not find it difficult to avoid their former sins, even if they had to remain watchful. Former alcoholics, for example, declared that their thirst had vanished. They now felt disgust at the sight of taverns that had formerly exerted an irresistible tug.

Perhaps the most exceptional characteristic of the awakening was its all-embracing scope. It did not give rise to two factions – the converted and the unconverted. On the contrary, partisanship dissipated. Almost without exception the movement took hold of everyone in the town. This was due in part to Blumhardt's manner. Factionalism and party strife did not flourish around him, and he made few enemies. His secret was that he trusted people – he had great confidence in the good inherent in every person. The changes he instigated, though dramatic, rarely led to hatred, quarreling, or persecution. When other preachers complained about being persecuted, he could be scathing: "Don't imagine this is happening because of your godliness. That is highly unlikely, since you don't have much of it anyway. If one of your listeners notices that you don't like him, he has reason to be angry with you."

The fact that no one was left out shows that the whole movement – the repentance as well as the peace people found – really was a work of God. Another sure sign was its longevity. From the beginning, Blumhardt feared the awakening would go the way of every other revival: "If this movement does not continue to grow and spread, and if the Holy Spirit is not continually poured out on us afresh, it is going to fizzle." To some extent, that did happen. But when you ask the descendants of those awakened in 1844 if that time has left no trace, their radiant eyes will provide the answer.

A report by Adolf Christ-Sarasin, town councilor of Basel and president of the Basel Mission Society, takes us into the year following the start of the awakening. On May 1, 1845 he attended the annual mission festival in Calw, and from there visited Möttlingen:

Calw was filled with people from the countryside, the townspeople completely crowded out by the peasants – an estimated six thousand people. From the terrace in front we looked down on the great marketplace and the crowd surging over it.

The appearance of Pastor Blumhardt from Möttlingen was the highlight of the festival. Everyone wanted to see him. Since the awakening in his congregation his name is on every mind and lip. He delivered his address with astonishing force; his passion infused and pervaded the whole gathering. A few of his questions capture the essence of his remarks: Are we really doomed to continue in so wretched a state? Must Christian life remain so beggarly poor? Why do even believers, on seeing the first stirrings of an awakening, say that not much of it will last? Why this lack of faith? Should not everything become new? According to Blumhardt something new must and will be given us when there is a fresh outpouring of the Spirit. We should pray for that. Then it will come, and we shall see great things, here among ourselves and in places far away.

After the festival I traveled with Blumhardt up to Möttlingen, about two hours from Calw in a high but fertile area. It was late when we drove into the village. At every house Blumhardt had reason to send up thanks to heaven. In this one a serious marital quarrel had ended; in that one a redeemed alcoholic was standing at the door; over here a rebellious teen had become obedient; over there, old enemies had mutually humbled themselves and become reconciled. From the lighted schoolhouse came the sound of lusty singing. About two hundred men had been singing together for half an hour while waiting for their pastor. We hurried there, and Blumhardt apologized for being late.

Blumhardt's interpretation of the daily text and the prayer were unique. There was something grand about his whole manner that reverberated in his voice. I felt this minister had a true inner connection with his listeners. Afterward, the schoolteacher related how his pupils had changed – how much better and more willingly they were now learning.

There are many personal stories worth mentioning. Some people's consciences were so heavily burdened by sin that it affected them physically. One man felt so constricted that when he spoke, he had trouble breathing and gasped with anxiety. Only when the pastor assured him, with the laying on of hands, that his sins were forgiven, did he sense relief.

Another parishioner, a rough character who had boasted that all this would never touch him, came one day and told Blumhardt, "The other day I came home, and before opening the door I heard my children praying for me so earnestly that I felt a heavy load descend on my heart. Now I have come for help." He, too, found peace.

At one meeting during the awakening, many of the villagers spoke openly of prayers being answered – particularly on the part of children. In every house married couples pray together on their knees.

Since the awakening, six elderly people in the parish found peace before they died; it was as if they had been spared to find a peace that stayed with them to the end. In each case, Blumhardt closed their eyes and sang a song of praise with those present.

Early the next morning I was in the village chatting with people, and spent an hour with Stanger. He is an elderly man, experienced and devout, and his impressions of the movement are important. Stanger's tears flowed with joy as he spoke of those newly awakened, and he assured me that their lives had been turned around. He himself had seen the change in several formerly difficult relatives.

Later that morning I accompanied Blumhardt to his weekly Bible study at the parish branch at Haugstett. Previously, hostile villagers had spitefully blocked a footpath that shortened his way from Möttlingen. Now they love him like a father. The mayor, who had been particularly hostile, was the first to appear at the school when the bell rang. It was ten o'clock on a fine morning but even so, some 150 people came and filled the room. They did not want to miss the Bible study.

Then Blumhardt talked about the people around Jesus: "Blind, lame, lepers – what a company Jesus chose! How it antagonized the wealthy! But it pleases us, doesn't it, to know that he associated with the poorest."

Later, while Blumhardt conversed with a few of the people, the schoolmaster told me that since the awakening the work in the fields has been going better. Previously, he said, there had been terrible cursing and swearing, but now everything is done peacefully and turns out well.

It was midday when we arrived back in Möttlingen, and people were sitting around their tables, but when they saw Blumhardt coming they got up and waved. I also saw the woman who had been possessed; she appeared to be entirely well.

Two other friends joined us in the rectory for dinner. Everything is very simple there, with pewter plates and spoons. There are four delightful children in the house, and Blumhardt's wife, Doris, who shares fully in her husband's work. In fact, the whole household cannot help being involved in Blumhardt's work, as there are often lines of people waiting to see him.

Blumhardt was not one to push people to repentance. When necessary, he could speak sharply. But "spiritual" attempts to force change through oratory or prayer made him shudder. The awakening had come of its own accord, and he would let its current carry him along at its own speed:

What I did was not anything I had sought, made, or forced, but something that came my way without my asking and completely undeserved. Actually, I was troubled, for I considered myself a sinner and could not imagine that God wanted to make an exception of me. I found it hard to grant absolution to others for sins I felt guilty of myself, and for which I had not yet been forgiven. Because I was pressed for time, I asked the Savior to consider these sins confessed, since he knew I was ready to do so at the next opportunity. Thus I was allowed to carry on with a temporarily reconciled conscience and a joyful spirit. Before long, a fellow minister provided the opportunity I desired.

The distress that met Blumhardt from those seeking peace was real and imperative, and as he grew to realize how general and widespread it was, he began to realize that the awakening had wider significance, not only for Christianity but also for all humankind.

Some in his position might have thought, "These things are possible only through someone like me" or, "I am not surprised at the effects of my efforts. I have what it takes." Such a person might have set about founding a new denomination and once again – as in countless times since the days of the apostles – tried to establish the "true Church of Christ."

Blumhardt opposed such narrow-minded arrogance with his whole being, and perhaps that is why he was granted so much. The awakening in Möttlingen led him to bolder hopes for the whole world, but also to deeper personal humility. When the great miracles came later, each one evoked in him a sense of startled awe. When others wanted to

extort similar answers to prayers – or kept recount-
ing instances where their prayers had been heard –
Blumhardt was apt to warn, "If you take it as a credit
to yourself even once, you can expect nothing
more," or, "Wanting a miracle for personal honor is
the greatest obstacle to ever receiving one."

He felt certain that his fellow ministers could –
and should – experience the same: "It's not as if *we*
possess anything. Our strength comes from the divine Word, which we must pass on unembellished."
How he longed for more openness in his fellow ministers when people seeking inner peace kept crowd-
ing in on him. As he wrote to Barth in April 1844:

> All they have to do is to announce in church that
> whoever feels burdened should come and see them.
> Oh, things must change, for I see clearly that what
> has been is nothing compared to what ought to be.

Later he wrote again:

> Everywhere consciences are waiting to be freed.
> People come streaming to me from all the villages
> around, and how happy I would be if I could say to
> them, "Go to your pastor!" I feel sorry for the
> people, but I am not allowed to do anything, and
> must turn them away. If only my Christian brothers
> had taken note of my concern…Oh, God knows
> how I feel, and how my heart burns for the whole
> world!

Despite the concern evident in this lament for people beyond his village, Blumhardt refused to encroach on other pastors' spheres of authority. Because of this and because of the cool and unsympathetic attitude of many of his colleagues, what could have been a universal movement gradually took on the appearance of a local phenomenon tied to his own person. The elemental power of repentance and forgiveness that had awakened and gripped thousands ended up being put down as "Blumhardt's special theory" and some of his theological friends almost regarded it as heresy. This grieved him tremendously. To him the awakening was an unquestionably auspicious event in God's history, and he had simply been the one to experience it firsthand.

Blumhardt took particular offense to charges that he was returning to Catholicism, for he was a Protestant through and through, and deeply rooted in Luther's spirit and writings. He held no animosity toward the Roman Catholic Church – it being one of the great historic forms of Christianity. But he knew that it was the abuse of the two main factors of the Möttlingen movement – confession and absolution – that had sparked the Reformation. Ever since then Protestants have been uncomfortable with these two features of church life, even though they are based on the words of Jesus: "Truly, I say to you, whatever you bind on earth shall be bound in heaven, and whatever you loose on earth shall be loosed in heaven" (Matt. 18:18).

———————

During the fight Blumhardt experienced something of the power with which Christ promises to work through his followers. At the time he had come to know that power as a warrior. Now he discovered it truly after the Savior's own heart: as a peacemaker – loving and reconciling. He saw how quickly and completely Christ forgives even heavy sins – murder, adultery, and theft – when they are brought to the light. And he saw how even flagrant sinners can find peace simply by confessing what burdens them.

But why the need to confess to another person? Is it not enough, to confess to God in secret? Certainly, it is important to consider all that is wrong in myself, before God to perceive it clearly and admit it to him – but God has actually known it all along. Only when something is confessed in the presence of somebody who does not yet know it, is the secret truly dragged out of the dark into the light of day.

The open manner of individuals and the wholesome tone of the gatherings in Möttlingen reflected the matter-of-fact nature of the awakening. Based as it was on repentance, there was nothing to feed spiritual pride. All who had participated in it had looked squarely at their past and opened themselves to someone else without reserve, and all were sure to be cured of any pious self-conceit for a long time. Those whose fervor had gained them a purely emotional peace, on the other hand, seemed to depend on an almost feverish degree of spirituality to keep them happy.

Blumhardt countered all criticism about confession with the evidence of Möttlingen:

> Certainly, confession can be misused. One can be hypocritical, can show off one's sin, can shamelessly blurt everything out like rowdies in a pub. One could even see confession as a good deed and feel righteous. But should the devil's corrupting of everything cause us to throw it all out?
>
> Christians sometimes fall into one heavy sin or another, and must be turned from pagans back into Christians. How is that to be done? Do you think one only needs to say, "I believe"? Certainly not! One needs to say, "I ought to repent." But how is one to do it? Weep for days, weeks, months, years while keeping one's guilt locked in one's heart? If we have become pagans, we must once again confess and receive forgiveness, just as at baptism. What can be clearer than that? No one can deny that such a new start brings extraordinary relief.

Blumhardt also discussed the question of absolution at length, because so many people viewed it as something they could only grant to themselves:

The effect of absolution on the people receiving it was such that they impressed everyone as completely changed persons. That was the main reason the movement kept spreading and finally encompassed both my villages.

In the case of about twelve persons, under the pressure of the moment, I granted absolution too early. These people, who had intentionally failed to bring out weighty wrongdoings, did not receive any relief through the act of absolution. Not only that; after each incident I felt tightness in my chest and some hours later a general fatigue, as if suddenly all my strength had gone. This general state of paralysis would last for two or three days. But then I recognized my error and ever since have remained cautious in granting absolution. I could have given it up altogether, but considered that cowardice. My experience made me all the more certain that there is something real to absolution, which I may not withhold from the souls entrusted to me.

Later that same summer I visited a distant colleague who lay mortally ill. He confessed to me and asked for absolution. I granted it to him as a favor to a friend (something completely out of place in matters concerning God) and arrived home sick in the way I just described. Thus I realized what a serious matter the authority granted by God is – that what we loose on earth shall be loosed in heaven.

What I have said might seem overly bold, but after granting absolution to nearly every member of my congregation its biblical foundation has become clear to me. In John 20:21–23 the risen Jesus tells his disciples, "As the Father has sent me, so I send you." Then he breathed on them and said, "Receive the Holy Spirit. If you forgive the sins of any, they are forgiven; if you retain the sins of any, they are retained."

Since this power is given by God, it may not be left idle and unused, or God will recall his gift. That would explain why Christianity has, for the most part, lost this remarkable power, which is useful and necessary for building up and preserving the Church. After all, hardly anyone believes in it or practices it.

A report from Dieterlen, an Alsatian manufacturer who visited Blumhardt shortly after the awakening and later became one of his closest friends, illustrates how the movement spread beyond Blumhardt's direct influence. Dieterlen was one of the first to pass on what he had received from Blumhardt through visits to Möttlingen and through lively correspondence. After his encounter with the awakening, he began to devote one day a week to caring for the sick in his own area. He served them with comforting words and with his money – his financial status permitted him to set out in the morning with a full purse and return with an empty one.

Dieterlen soon noticed that some of the sick, when they caught sight of him through the window, would grab the nearest devotional book and open it. So, after Blumhardt's own fashion, he tried to foster a more natural and brotherly relationship with those he visited:

> When people I meet for the first time start walking along on pious stilts, I stick to the mundane and talk about their debts, their goats, and their manure, until they come down from their heights. It is wrong to burst in with edification right away. If you pounce on people with Bible reading and prayer, the honest become shy, the bad laugh, and the weak play-act.

In this manner, Dieterlen awakened something in many, giving them reason to believe again and courage to repent and turn around. He told of a poor family living several hours' walking distance from his village:

> I found a consumptive, dejected woman, a man who tried to drown his misery in drink, six children in rags, and a messy, disorderly house. I showed the people compassion, repeated my visits, won their confidence, and was able to speak to their hearts. One day the man told me, "You see, sir, everybody has left us in our misery for so long, that we began to think, 'No one cares; even God has forsaken us.' We let ourselves sink lower and lower. Then you came, and came again, and we thought, 'Here is a stranger who visits us and keeps coming. And if a stranger has not forsaken us, then God has not forsaken us either, and there is still hope.' And so we found new trust in God."

IV MIRACLES

If the fight and the movement of repentance it sparked were of significance for the kingdom of God, as Blumhardt felt certain, then the miracles that followed held equally rich promise. Blumhardt saw each of these events as an organic outgrowth of the one before – and heard God speaking through them with an unmistakable certainty.

Already in the winter of 1844, when the people of Möttlingen came weeping to the rectory, some of them experienced the unexpected healing of their physical ailments, as well as inner peace. One, a man who suffered so severely from rheumatism in one thigh that he often fell, was healed after confession. When Blumhardt laid hands on him as a sign of forgiveness, he felt something slide from his thigh and pass out of his body, and from that moment on he felt completely well. At first he did not quite believe his good fortune, and kept quiet while he waited for the next bad spell. But it never came; his rheumatism seemed gone for good. Many such miracles came to Blumhardt's attention. Each one encouraged and reassured him, particularly since the controversy over his pastoral work had isolated him from his fellow ministers, as described in the preceding chapter.

In confessions, Blumhardt's parishioners often told him of superstitious attempts – from sorcery to subtler forms of "sympathetic" magic – to find cures for their aches and pains. This disturbed him deeply. During the fight he had acquired a horror of all such practices, and come to feel that any help attained by them violated the authority of God and gave honor to opposing powers. Yet when Blumhardt urged people to reject these practices, they would often ask him, "But what are we to do? The doctor lives far away, and when bleeding or any other such emergency must be dealt with, we can not wait. Besides, we are too poor to call the doctor anyway."

To this Blumhardt would reply with confidence, "The Savior will do more for you than the devil has. Of course, it is always good to consider whether or not what has befallen you might be punishment for something you have done. But if it is, don't give up. Pray! And if you let me know about it, I will pray with you and for you." Recalling one instance that encouraged him to proceed in this direction, Blumhardt wrote:

One morning a mother came rushing in, beside herself. She had accidentally spilled boiling oatmeal on her three-year-old and did not know what to do. I hurried over and found the child scalded all over its body and screaming. The room filled with people, and before long someone offered that so-and-so knew a spell and should be sent for right away. But I could not allow that. Offering a few words of consolation, I asked the people to become silent and pray. Then I took the child in my arms and sighed. Immediately it grew quiet and calm and no longer seemed to feel the least pain, even though the burns only disappeared several days later.

After that, instances of divine help began to occur one after the other. The parents of a child with a severe eye disease had consulted a doctor, who declared an operation essential. Shrinking from this prospect, they went to Calw to ask their former pastor, Barth, whether they should let the child be operated on or take him to Pastor Blumhardt. Barth answered, "If you have faith that the Savior can and will heal your child, by all means go to Blumhardt. But if you do not have such faith, then accept the operation."

"We do have faith," they said, and made a visit to Blumhardt, after which the eye improved so much that the child's sight was fully restored after three days.

Before long word spread and people outside Blumhardt's congregation began to flock to him in search of physical healing. Every week new people came, and they went away thanking God for the help they had received. Infirmities of all kinds vanished: eye problems, tuberculosis, eczema, arthritis, and more. Similar miracles happened within the rector's own household, though these were kept quiet. A person who was there at the time later said, "There were so many miracles that I can no longer recall the details. We felt the Lord's nearness so tangibly that they seemed natural, and no one made a great deal of it."

One Sunday a young man from a village an hour's walk away carried his younger brother, a hunchback, to Möttlingen. When they came again the following Sunday, both of them walked, though the boy was still quite deformed. A short time later, however, he was straight and healthy. When asked what had happened, he said simply, "I had something on my back, but now it's gone."

One day a university student came whose eyes were so bad that he had to be led about, and so light-sensitive that even dim candlelight caused him pain. It was a Saturday, the day Blumhardt held a weekly evening service known for its intimate character, and Blumhardt invited the young man to listen in from the dark sacristy. This the man did, and when a light was carried through the sacristy to him at the end of the service, it no longer bothered him. By Sunday morning he was seeing so well that he could walk unaided.

At Easter a garrulous young man with tuberculosis came to Möttlingen from a considerable distance, certain that he would find healing during the holidays, even though his doctor had given up on him. Before the Sunday service, it seemed that nothing could silence him, but afterward he grew pensive. The sermon had pierced his heart like an arrow and he murmured to himself, "I have got to change; I must see the pastor." Later, broken and quiet, he made his way to Blumhardt's study. In the evening he appeared again, cheerful and healthy. He stayed another day, then traveled home and resumed work – at the same unhealthy occupation the doctor had declared to be the cause of his illness in the first place. There he remained well, indeed, so happy that he sang while he worked, and held his own in every way until he died two years later of unknown causes. "He became like an angel," an acquaintance said of him.

A lady who had sought treatment at one spa after another – she had a paralyzing spinal infection – came to Möttlingen in the summer of 1846 and took lodging in a farmhouse near the rectory. Every Sunday she had someone carry her to the church-yard so she could listen to Blumhardt's sermon. On the second or third Sunday she was there, he gave a sermon on Zacchaeus, and he spoke of two stages of conversion:

> First, there is the awakening: Zacchaeus wants to reach Jesus at any cost and will not let anything turn him aside. He climbs a tree, disregarding all ridicule. There he discovers that Jesus is in fact looking for

him. Zacchaeus is overwhelmed by the kindness and love shown when Jesus, opening himself to the grumbling of his own followers, forgives and accepts Zacchaeus. Many people get that far.

Second, there is the conversion: Most who reach the first stage think they have reached the goal. If they were in Zacchaeus' place, they would snub the mutterers and gloat over the attention they had received. But to acknowledge the validity of the reproaches, to change, and to make restitution – that they do not consider necessary. Having been pardoned, they become puffed-up instead of humble. Zacchaeus, on the other hand, admits that the grumblers are justified, and promises to pay back everyone he has cheated, thus proving that Jesus was right to pardon him. Only then does Jesus say of him, "Today salvation has come to this house."

The sick lady thought Blumhardt had preached the sermon especially for her, and remained in the churchyard to listen to the services that followed. After dinner the next day she begged him to visit her, and poured out her heart to him, without mentioning her illness at all.

At five o'clock in the afternoon, Blumhardt was just setting out for a stroll with the rectory guests when the lady's attendant hurried up to him in tears and said, "I don't mean to take you by surprise, sir, but my mistress is walking!" They all set out at once for the lady's lodging, and sure enough, there she was, walking out to meet them at the top of the stairs. Everyone gathered in her room and knelt down to thank God.

––––––––

Miracles involving mentally disturbed individuals were often dramatic, which may be reason to tell of such cases sparingly, but one story including both physical and mental healing deserves to be recounted at length:

A wealthy woman had been thrown into a state of depression by her husband's sudden death and was plagued by suicidal tendencies. She came to Möttlingen with her mother. At first she stayed at an inn, but following a suicide attempt, the proprietor refused to let her stay. Moved by compassion, Blumhardt agreed to take her into his rectory. He gave her a room and provided an attendant, to whom he gave strict instructions not to leave the woman alone day or night.

The sick woman was not at all religious, and had no stomach for Blumhardt's prayer meetings. Like many of the mentally ill, she also had an outspoken personal dislike for him. Still, she agreed to stay – so desperate was she for his help. One morning, while in a nearby room, Hans heard a suspicious noise from the widow's room and called for her attendant.

Hearing no reply, he looked for her and found her downstairs, where she had just gone to fetch water.

"Come quick. Something is wrong!" Hans cried.

Together they ran upstairs and, finding the door locked, rushed down and out into the street. From there they looked up to see an open window, and the widow hanging by her neck from the crossbar. Running back inside, Hans smashed the door with an axe and took the lifeless body down. The blows awakened Blumhardt and others, who came running. Blumhardt helped Hans loosen the scarf with which the woman had hanged herself, and they laid her on a bed.

Diligent attempts were made to revive her, but it was to no avail. Still Blumhardt refused to admit defeat, "This must not be. Let us pray!" With that he and his wife Doris, Gottliebin, and Hans knelt down and prayed. Next, Blumhardt asked Hans to hold open the woman's mouth, and he breathed into it. After first the woman drew a few breaths; then she seemed lifeless again, finally she broke into a drawn-out, wolf-like howl.

Blumhardt had already notified the district physician by special messenger. When the doctor arrived, he listened to woman's howling, examined her (she was still unconscious) and declared that she was as good as dead. As for her continued howling, he claimed that it could be understood as an expression of pain, but not as a sign that she would recover.

He then left the house, having apparently given up hope. The woman relapsed into a coma. Hans remained by her side. Later, during evening devotions, the singing woke her. With a pleased expression on her face she said, "The pastor is such a nice man!" Then, turning to Hans she said, "You are here, too, Fritz?" (Fritz was the name of her deceased husband.)

"Yes," he replied, somewhat embarrassed but trying not to upset her in any way.

"Oh," she said, "it's good that you are back, too! Like you I had died. I was in hell, but Blumhardt, the good man, has called me back. I don't want to go there again."

Hans spoke to her gently, and she gradually calmed down. At ten o'clock Mose and another man came to relieve Hans. This agitated her.

"Go away, go away! I don't want to return to hell." Then, to Hans, "They want to take me back there! You will stay, Fritz, won't you?"

The men left and Hans stayed, but for a long time she remained anxious that she might be taken back to hell. Finally, Hans decided to try a little ruse.

"Dear wife," he said, "don't you think it would be better for you to be quiet now and try to get a little sleep?"

"Yes, thank you, Fritz, you might be right," she replied, and before long sank into healthy sleep. When she woke again at five the next morning, she said, "Are you there, Mr. Dittus?"

"Yes."

"How odd that I took you for my husband, before!"

At this Hans admonished her, asking, "Do you realize what you did yesterday? How could you do such a thing as to take your life!"

"Yes, I know it well. It was my greed. When my husband was alive we put aside a thousand florins every year, and I could not get over the fact that this had come to an end. That's why I wanted to kill myself. I kept thinking, 'If only the maid would go out for a moment!' and all night something in me said, 'See that scarf? You could hang yourself with that.' But I shall not do that again. I know now where suicide leads. I was in hell, and I don't want to go there again. Oh, the pastor is a good man!" Before long, she was completely well in body, soul, and spirit. She remarried three months later and remained an active member of the parish.

In some cases, Blumhardt noted, a sick person's weakness might lead him to commit a deranged act, despite his firm resolve to control himself and find healing. Such a person, Blumhardt said, was not incurably sick even if severely disturbed: "In the biblical sense, every person's spirit – that which is holy and of God – is immortal, and what cannot die cannot be ill either."

It was this faith that made Blumhardt accept even the most bizarre guests, such as the man who arrived at the rectory turning somersaults. He had apparently come in this manner all the way from Calw. He, too, found healing.

During church services, the sacristy usually contained an odd assortment of people, including epileptics and the mentally disturbed. Blumhardt made this area available so as to shield these sufferers from expressions of shock or exaggerated pity from the healthy attendees of his services. Still, he demanded that compassion and understanding be shown toward the sick. "Don't be shocked by odd occurrences or make too much of them. Instead, pray for those whom you see having an attack."

As for the main hall of the church, it was not entirely closed to the mentally ill. Blumhardt wanted his congregation to see itself as a fighting church, and to help those who suffered by interceding in prayer. Sometimes this was necessary right in the middle of a worship service. Once a man got up in the middle of the sermon and began to recite blasphemous doggerel at which Blumhardt had the congregation start a hymn. The man quieted down. Another time an epileptic was seized with severe convulsions and then collapsed as if dead. Naturally the people nearest him wanted to pick him up, but Blumhardt told them to leave him alone and pray for him instead, and he continued to preach. Eventually the man came to and got up on his own.

Blumhardt's welcoming attitude to disturbed visitors exposed him to occasional risks, as was the case with people whose illness caused them to act violently. One time a burly man sitting near the pulpit worked himself into such a frenzy that he got up and threatened to throw Blumhardt out of the pulpit. Hans, who had a way with such people, quickly calmed him.

Two stories Blumhardt recounted himself involved illnesses caused by false piety. While still in the nursery, a boy had begun, half playfully, to preach to his brothers and sisters. His parents listened admiringly, which egged him on. Over the years he preached more and more earnestly and solemnly. In the end, he even turned on his parents and preached repentance to them, at which they dissolved in tears. Other people took notice too, and flocked to hear the little prophet, who soon became quite a sensation. All of a sudden an inexplicable malady put an end to the prophetic glory: the boy was struck dumb. A physician, unable to help, advised the parents to take the boy to Blumhardt. When Blumhardt learned what had transpired, he thundered at the boy, "What is the fifth commandment?" No answer. He repeated the question emphatically, until the boy managed to stammer, "Honor your father and your mother." Then Blumhardt scolded him indignantly, particularly for daring to preach to his parents: "If God wants repentance preached to your parents, he certainly won't use you to do it." After this the boy recovered quickly.

In the other case a woman came to Blumhardt's study with the question, "Tell me what you think of visions and revelation. In Sunday school yesterday I noticed that you seem to mistrust them. But I think you err." She then told him she had been sick most of her life and unable to work, but during the last couple of years God had comforted her with a wonderful form of compensation: a bright light that surrounded her almost constantly. In this light she at times saw Jesus and heard him speak to her or to God the Father, and now and then she would hear the Father reply to the Son.

As Blumhardt listened he sensed an aura of strange spirituality around the woman and remembered hearing that she was regarded as an uncommonly gifted seer. Suddenly it came to him: that there was something seriously amiss, and he bluntly cut off the woman by telling her: "That's all from the devil!" at which she stormed out of the room.

A day later, however the woman came back in tears to thank Blumhardt for healing her. When she had left him, she said, she had felt angry and hurt, but from that moment on her bright light was gone, and she was given the humility to recognize that it had all had been sickness and deceit – the fruits of unbounded spiritual pride.

Since these accounts relate the miracles of Möttlingen back to back, without the context of the daily life in which they occurred, they do not tell the whole story. That, in a word, is the simple fact that God was such a constant and intimate presence in the parish, that people were able to simply bring their needs before him in a repentant and believing spirit, and just as quietly and simply receive his help time and again.

In February 1846 Blumhardt wrote to a like-minded colleague about a malady of his own:

> Sometimes you just have to accept it when your ailments do not go away quickly. All last summer I had a cough and a sore throat, and such trouble with my shoulder joint that I could hardly use my arm. I prayed, but healing cannot be forced by prayer. So I put up with it, hoping it would eventually go, and now it is gone.

In their simple way, the people of Möttlingen committed everything to God – including hardships caused by disease among farm animals. Blumhardt explained:

> Are not cattle part of "our daily bread?" We pray for bread in the Lord's Prayer, so why not pray for the cattle to be preserved? It may seem strange to you and me, but not to the peasant, for whom, unfortunately, a calf is often of greater value than a child. After all, they are only praying – kneeling down in a corner of the stable and saying the Lord's Prayer, and that is all. But the beasts improve at once. I can cite many instances where help has been received in this way.

Every now and then, cattle may be tormented by demons and if this seems strange, it ought to be remembered that Jesus sent demons into a herd of pigs. People are liable to ascribe this to witches and turn to witchcraft for a solution, but I discourage that. I assure them that the best help against demons – if they stand right otherwise – is the Lord's Prayer.

Despite such dramatic occurrences, it remains that the faith of Blumhardt's parishioners was in fact simple and straightforward. Anyone tempted to imitate them should not forget that it was through judgment and repentance that they found such exceptional recourse to divine protection.

Not surprisingly, Blumhardt's influence was a considerable nuisance for the local authorities. More than a few clerics and physicians complained that he was infringing on their rights. Besides, until 1848, the state government displayed such a marked aversion to "pietism" that lively expression of Christianity other than that sanctioned by the established church hierarchy was looked at with suspicion.

These difficulties were eased in two ways: for the authorities, by Blumhardt's tact, and for Blumhardt through his various friendly associations. Blumhardt had a keen sense of his obligations toward governmental authority. He guarded against pressure from hotheads who urged him to "obey God more than men." Though he could hold his own position valiantly in questions of conscience, he always tried to view things from the perspective of the authorities, and his sincerity and respect reduced the danger of unnecessary conflict and gained him the generous trust of his clerical superiors.

Something that further helped Blumhardt's name, right to the highest government levels – and stood him in good stead later on – was a visit from the King of Württemberg. It happened this way: One Sunday morning two strange gentlemen walked into town and checked in at The Ox. Later they came to the church service and chose seats next to the organ – not the best location, as the organist was hard of hearing and made astonishing demands on his instrument and on his listeners' ears. Shortly after this an army recruit who had come from Stuttgart on furlough said to Hans, "You know that gentleman up there next to the organ? That's the king!"

After the service, in the study, Hans told Blumhardt that the King had attended the morning service and through the window pointed out the man, who was strolling through the rectory garden. Blumhardt answered, "You might be right," but he did nothing further, respecting his visitor's apparent wish to remain incognito. The man attended the afternoon service as well, and in the evening a stately carriage pulled up and took him away.

Though this encounter (and similar ones involving other government officials) probably shielded Blumhardt from severe official censure, obstacles were put in his way. In January 1846 the ministry forbade him to "include healing as part of his pastoral duty instead of directing people to the medical profession." Blumhardt answered with a twelve-page document, which ended, "I shall no longer lay my hands on any stranger, nor let any stay here over the weekend. In short, I shall do no more than listen to their complaints, maybe give them some advice, and then let them go. But if miracles continue – for God will not let his hands be tied – and people continue to flock here, let no one charge me with disobedience."

In May of the same year Blumhardt accepted another considerable restriction in an effort to appease his embarrassed superiors. In a letter dated June 18, 1846, he told a friend:

> Things are going forward despite an outward hitch. About four weeks ago I stopped allowing people to tell me of their ailments, and since then I have had to refuse seeing strangers privately at all. They have to be satisfied with attending my church services. I am doing this voluntarily, because otherwise I might lose everything. In spite of it all, much is still happening in the church, though the stream of sick people has fallen off considerably.

Around the same time he announced from the pulpit one day that he had promised not to accept visitors from outside Möttlingen into the rectory. But his matter-of-factness betrayed how heartbreakingly difficult was for him to accept his new restrictions:

> You sick ones, just come to church, lay your suffering before the Savior, and listen carefully to the sermon. You are assured of my intercession and that of the congregation. There is no need for me to know your specific ailments.

People who had not heard the announcement kept coming, and when Hans would have to turn them away, Blumhardt's eyes filled with tears: "The poor people! Gentlemen, officers, students, merchants – no one stops them. But the poor are not allowed in, they just get pushed around." Of course, it wasn't just ignorance of Blumhardt's prohibition that kept his visitor's coming. Many of them simply felt they *had* to see Blumhardt, and nothing would stop them.

One day a peasant who had somehow managed to slip through the front door started up the stairs. Blumhardt ordered him back.

"But, Mr. Blumhardt," the man countered, "there is nothing wrong with me now. I only wanted to thank you."

"Well, that's fine."

"It is true that I had something wrong with me, a whole lot. There was…"

"Well, I don't want to know what it was. But you did have something wrong with you?"

"Yes, and I did exactly as you said. I came to your service and listened carefully, and now I am fine."

For those who couldn't get through, Hans served as an unofficial liaison. No one had ordered him to close his ears to the people's needs. And the next time he found himself in Blumhardt's study, it was natural that he should share the things that filled his mind and heart. Yet given its roundabout route, such channels of communication between Blumhardt and his visitors were not enough to result in accusations of infraction.

Still, a certain amount of friction between Blumhardt and the church authorities was inevitable. The consistory (under pressure from physicians, clergymen, and journalists) and Blumhardt (facing the tide of people's misery) could hardly be expected to arrive at a common point of view. The widely accepted view of the day was that bodies should be entrusted the care of physicians only, whereas clergy should stick to purely spiritual concerns. The consistory, sworn to uphold that dichotomy, frowned on any evidence that faith could influence physical recovery, particularly when that evidence was conspicuous and recurring. In their eyes, Blumhardt was willfully disturbing this harmonious division of responsibilities. They informed him that the role of religion was simply to console – to emphasize the blessing brought by suffering and the value of patience.

Actually, Blumhardt never sought to compete with anyone. In a report to one government official he wrote, "It was never my intention to treat mental illness. The people who come seeking my help are burdened souls who do not find the strength, either from within or without, to free themselves. The only remedy I use is an awakening of trust in God, and confident prayer to him." As for physicians, he made it clear that he expected people to make use of whatever medical assistance they could:

> The rejection of medical help, especially of surgery, is completely wrong. It is a mistake to reduce prayer to a singular method of curing illness. Healing powers are simply lacking in our time, so why not make use of the help people can render one another with the training and experience they have? Rejection of such help springs from self-will, and from an impudence that wants to exact everything from God, whether he is willing or not.

However, when the consistory demanded that Blumhardt turn all supplicants away – not only from his own person, but also from any hope of direct help from God – Blumhardt could no longer obey, especially when faced with infirmities that had baffled physicians. He had, on one the hand, recourse to Scriptures that confirmed his experiences and actions, and on the other hand, his civic freedom, which entitled him, like any other citizen, to let his convictions guide his actions. He declared that no minister had ever been asked to comply with such a demand. To be sure, the consistory's request that he forbid strangers to stay in Möttlingen overnight was an extraordinary and rather unrealistic demand to make on a minister.

Blumhardt intended to obey the established order, but his compliance with this decree was naturally somewhat elastic, and caused him an official reprimand for disobedience in front of two colleagues called as witnesses.

At least one friendly encounter with the medical profession reassured Blumhardt during this time of increased restriction. One weekend in the spring of 1846, a skeptical medical student named Steinkopf came to Möttlingen from Stuttgart to investigate the miracles. Avoiding the rectory, he took up lodgings at The Ox. After the Sunday morning service, he burst in excitedly on a cluster of young men from various regions of Germany. He said he had just met a former patient of the Tübingen clinic, whom they had discharged as incurable, outside the church. When he greeted her with, "Well, Magdalena, are you here, too?" she had replied, "Yes, of course. I was cured here!" She told him that in December 1845, when Blumhardt could still work unhindered, she had seen him two or three times after church, and had told him of her illness and how it was going.

Steinkopf, amazed, invited Magdalena to come with him to the rectory, introduced himself, and declared his purpose for coming to Möttlingen. Then, asking for a room he examined the patient, though only after receiving Blumhardt's permission to do so. His findings were set down in the following document:

In March 1844, Maria Magdalena Rapp from Enzthal near Wildbad, thirty-five years of age, was accepted into the medical clinic at Tübingen, as she suffered from pemphigus. She was treated with various remedies, but the blisters, though often disappearing for a few days, would always break out again on different parts of the body. The application of arsenic caused the blisters to vanish, and for some days the patient was free of them.

Then, in the winter of 1844, serious vomiting of blood, bloody stools, and stomach pains set in. From then on – doubtless in consequence of a chronic stomach inflammation – the patient could not ingest any kind of warm food. The spells of blood-vomiting recurred every three to five weeks. Several times, the patient was very close to death. The pemphigus reappeared with all its earlier persistence.

Rapp was discharged in July 1845 as a completely hopeless case, according to the judgment of all physicians observing her. As a last resort she tried the mineral baths at Wildbad for some weeks, but without any success. Her condition remained unchanged until December, when she went to Möttlingen to seek help from Pastor Blumhardt. After her first visit she already felt much better. After she had seen the pastor once or twice more, her symptoms began to disappear and by May 1846 the undersigned found the patient in Möttlingen, where she was attending church, fully restored to health.

A detailed history of Rapp's illness can be found in the Tübingen clinic, where – after protracted and unsuccessful treatment – she had been declared completely incurable.

The truth of the above is attested by

K. Steinkopf, medical candidate
Möttlingen, May 24, 1846

Another episode that took place around the same time involved a woman with a convulsively clenched hand, which had also been treated without success in Tübingen. She arrived on a Saturday and wanted to see Blumhardt, but was turned away. However, Blumhardt heard of her infirmity through Hans and told him to invite her to the evening service. The following morning, seeing Hans she marched triumphantly across the rectory yard and declared, "Now I must see the pastor!"

"I know, dear lady, but it's just not possible."

"Why not?" she retorted, stretching out her hand – open, flat, and completely cured. She told him that her hand had opened the day before during the evening devotions. Unfortunately the woman later went back to Tübingen to show off her hand to those who had treated her there. Regarded as an impostor,

she was not given a very friendly reception, which upset her greatly. Blumhardt, hearing of her indignation, advised her, "Go home, be quiet, and first make a
fresh start yourself."

This case had unpleasant consequences for Blumhardt. For one thing, the woman, though unmarried
had several children, a circumstance that made her
cure offensive to some. For another, she caused
Blumhardt considerable embarrassment because of
the boastful and sensational way in which she adver-
tised her healing. Some of what she said was true.
Blumhardt, in greeting her in church, had taken
hold of her crippled hand in an expression of sympathy and blessing. But embellished as it was by her
colorful description, the miracle was quickly misconstrued and cited as a breach of promise on
Blumhardt's part. In the course of her publicity
seeking – perhaps because of it – her affliction returned, which added to the critical misgivings.

Such reversal of healing did occur at times, and
though it pained Blumhardt, it did not surprise him.
He regarded any divine help he received merely as a
foretaste of what was to come. Sometimes though,
as in this case, a relapse seemed related to a mis-
understanding of the help received – that is, treating
an instance of healing as if it were Blumhardt's doing and not God's.

In a letter to his friend Dieterlen, who was swamped
by a flood of sick people asking him to contact Blum-

hardt for them, Blumhardt wrote about the help given to seemingly unworthy people:

> I wonder, when people suffer a relapse, whether it is intended to lead them into a deeper, more inward state. With so many sick people coming, there are bound to be those who arrive with a more superficial approach. The Lord does his part, but in turn demands something from them.
>
> But what about people who are bad? My experience is that the Savior pays little attention to that. It surprises me how many times the worst are given the most, and often much more quickly than others. Why? Perhaps they are more humble and broken… Oh, the loving kindness of the Lord – free of charge and totally undeserved!

The influx of visitors dropped off considerably after Blumhardt agreed to deny personal talks, which were, after all, the essence of what Möttlingen represented and offered. His words of comfort, admonition, rebuke, and forgiveness to individuals were imbued with a rare power. God had endowed him with a special ability to help others – and not only by healing. Many received clarity in personal problems, direction for their vocation, strength to carry responsibilities, or an easing of difficult circumstances. People's need for true pastoral care, which slumbers unrecognized in thousands, had powerfully awakened. Naturally, once someone benefited from Blumhardt's counsel, he wanted more – for himself and for his relatives, friends, and foes. But now this place of refuge and hope, compassion and peace was closed.

To some extent Blumhardt's counsel was still available to anyone who took in the advice he gave from the pulpit. But in the long run this impersonal form of communication did not satisfy most people, and Möttlingen lost its main appeal, which could not be found just anywhere: unconditional love, blunt honesty, and wholesome comfort. Möttlingen grew even quieter during the economic recession of 1847 and the political turmoil of 1848.

While Blumhardt's direct contact with peasants outside his congregation dropped off, his pastoral work continued with people from the upper classes who still had money to travel. His household always included long-term guests in need of help. One of these guests, a woman who stayed with Blumhardt at Bad Boll many years later, offered the following testimony:

> As a young girl I was afflicted with a severe eye dis-
> ease. At the advice of famous doctors I was sub-
> jected to several courses of treatment so drastic that
> they made me sick for years. For a while I was hardly
> alive. I slowly recovered from the effects of the
> medicines, but as my general health improved, my
> sight grew worse. After long indecision I decided to
> consult a doctor once again. He offered no prospect
> of recovery, giving me only slim hope that further

deterioration might be halted if I gave up occupations such as reading, writing, and knitting.

I had heard Pastor Blumhardt preach, and felt drawn to him, without having more precise information about his work. I sensed only that here was a place to find help in my dejected state. I inquired and, unexpectedly, received an invitation to come and stay for half a year. While my eyes did not improve, there they did not get worse either, and I found strength to carry my affliction.

Two years later, I returned in much the same state, unable to make myself useful in any way. One day Blumhardt asked me if my family would like me to seek medical advice again. I had to answer yes, but added that I was resolved not to do so, since previous treatments had had such a devastating effect. "You shouldn't say that," he said. "You just like it too much here. That is why you shy away from doctors. Why shouldn't you believe that your eyes can be helped? I know a famous oculist in Stuttgart who is a good friend. Why not let him give you one more checkup?"

We traveled to Stuttgart, and I will never forget how Blumhardt, seated in an armchair, followed the examination with lively interest. The doctor's verdict: "There is nothing that can be done. Drugs would only speed up the loss of sight. The optic nerves are worn out, and the muscles and mucous membranes are so weak they barely function. It's a marvel that there is still any sight left at all." This agreed in every detail with the other doctors' conclusions.

On the train returning home Blumhardt asked me, "Are you sad, my child?"

"Oh, no," I replied, "I already knew all that. I was just afraid the doctor would want to attempt an operation."

"Well," he said, "I think you know that where people can do nothing, the Savior enters with his help. Now you must simply hold out in faith and hope."

Since that day nine years have passed, and I have not gone blind. I am still extremely short-sighted, but my eyes have improved marvelously. I feel no pain, my exaggerated sensitivity to light has gone, and with the aid of glasses I can read and write all day and live like anyone else. Whenever the condition worsened, I would mention it to Blumhardt, personally or in writing, and before long help would come again. Indeed, the Savior has done great things for me.

On his journeys, Blumhardt was constantly surrounded by people pleading for help. A factory worker living about an hour's walk from Elberfeld was afflicted with a painful dermatological condition. He had already expended every prospect of medical help, when he was told that a well-known pastor had come to Elberfeld, and that through his intercession many people had been cured of serious illnesses. The man, who did not think much of "pious gentlemen," resolved to see for himself.

Arriving at Elberfeld, he found Blumhardt, and began to unfold his tale of woe. Blumhardt, quickly perceiving the problem, said, "My dear friend, I have no time right now, though I can see you need help. Just attend the service and listen carefully, and may the Savior help you!" The man could scarcely conceal his anger at being treated so curtly. He grumbled to himself, "There's the compassionate Blumhardt for you! That's just what religious people are like. And now he expects me to go to church!" But he decided to attend the service anyway, hoping Blumhardt would say something that addressed his condition. And in fact, although the man did not catch on, Blumhardt did: he preached on the text, "Ask, and you will receive." After the service, half encouraged, half enraged, he turned his back on the church and set off for home. "Those pious people and their compassion!" he fumed – but the words of the sermon kept echoing in his head.

Suddenly he became aware of a strange sensation in his skin. Starting from a number of points, it kept spreading and growing stronger. Skeptical but curious, he hurried home, locked himself in his room, and examined himself. To his amazement he discovered that the disease was indeed rapidly disappearing. The man kept his excitement to himself until he was certain of the result, but later he hurried back to Elberfeld and through acquaintances relayed the good news to Blumhardt.

Several memorable personal experiences from the summer of 1844 stayed with Blumhardt for life. Once, while walking back with some fellow ministers from a festival in a neighboring village, he composed the following verse, which he shared with his companions:

Jesus is victorious King,
Who over all his foes has conquered.
Jesus, soon the world will fall
At his feet, by love overpowered.
Jesus leads us with his might
From the darkness to radiant light.

While singing the verse to a well-known melody, it seemed that hundreds of voices in the nearby woods suddenly joined in, so powerfully that at least one of the men, flabbergasted, stopped singing. Blumhardt, however, went on singing lustily. When he arrived home, he was met by Gottliebin, who recited for him the very same verse he had just composed and sung!

Blumhardt told of several instances of divine protection when hostile attempts were made on his life. In general, he seldom made enemies, but his campaign against superstition and magic did earn him the deadly enmity of a few, and at least one plot to murder him came to light. For a time the police even assigned a nightly patrol to his house.

During July 1844 the Blumhardts heard footsteps along the halls of their house every night, even though the building was searched each evening and the entrances bolted. Since the disturbance never went any further, they got used to it, even when – as one night – they heard all kinds of noises from the adjoining barn.

Blumhardt's mother was visiting, and a carriage had been ordered for her departure the next morning. A coachman, arriving early, noticed smoke billowing from the barn door, and sizing up the situation, ran through the village shouting, "Fire!" Soon the yard was filled with neighbors carrying a motley assortment of water containers.

The innkeeper of The Ox took charge of the brigade and gave orders to put out any flames that might break out when he opened the barn door. Then he forced the door open, exposing a burning heap of straw, which was quickly extinguished. Inside they found various indications of arson scattered throughout the barn, including dozens of packs of matches and a number of long beanpoles placed in a tub with their tips pointing to the floor of Blumhardt's bedroom above. They were already charred at the bottom. Only Blumhardt remained unruffled by the hubbub. When everyone was gathered again back in the house, he read the scheduled

Bible text for the day: "No weapon made to harm you will prevail" (Isa. 54:17).

That same month the riddle of the nightly stalker was solved. It happened like this. One night, hearing a noise directly over his bedroom, Blumhardt shouted, "Jesus is the victor." The following morning – Blumhardt's birthday – someone found a letter stuck under the back door, scribbled in pencil on a scrap of paper. Dated July 16, 1844, it read:

Dear friends,

I am leaving your house at four in the morning, but not as the man I was when I came in. I came as a murderer with murderous thoughts, until I heard the shout, "Jesus is the victor." Yes, Jesus is victorious, and now my conscience has awakened. I spent the rest of the night in despair among the roof timbers. Your efforts have been in vain, though, for the devil has been thwarting you. Unless the blood of Christ cries out mightily even today, all that is left for me to do is to take the knife I wanted to pierce your heart with and turn it against my own breast. God's flaming eye has seen me; he has stabbed my heart…I will receive what my deeds deserve. I have served the devil loyally, and hell is his reward for me now. When I heard the name of the Most High called out, something went right through me. It made me so docile that now I only want to let you see me as I am. Be kind enough to intercede for me with the heavenly Father.

I thank you for your faithfulness. Think of me for Jesus' sake.

Your enemy

The signature was illegible, but when Blumhardt brought the letter to his Bible class that evening, passing on the author's plea for prayers, someone identified him as a man from a nearby village.

One afternoon Blumhardt went to Haugstett for a Bible class. Worried by the recent attempts on her husband's life, Doris sent Hans to meet him so he would not have to come home alone in the dark. Blumhardt, rankled at the idea of needing a protector, said that Doris must have forgotten there was a full moon. But her precaution paid off.

Suddenly two men appeared at the edge of the woods. At first, Blumhardt took them for peasants returning late from their fields and then, seeing their weapons gleam in the moonlight, for hunters. Just then the men took aim at Blumhardt, who quickly cried out, "Jesus is the victor." At this they immediately lowered their rifles. Later, in the middle of the forest they were surprised by another gunman, who raised his rifle and cocked the hammer. Hans was ready to dive for cover, but Blumhardt restrained him and prayed aloud for their would-be assassin, who lowered his gun. Coming out of the woods, they again met two armed men half-hidden in the meadow. Hans, by now feeling invincible, shouted, "Go ahead! Pull the trigger. It won't go off!" At this the gunmen, evidently strangers come from a distance, lowered their weapons and went harmlessly on their way.

Wilhelm Hofacker, a minister and close friend of Blumhardt, wrote of one of his most memorable experiences:

> I once attended the main Sunday service in Möt-tlingen. It was summer, right before harvest. I was seated in front, in one of the pews reserved for honored guests. The church was crammed with listeners, and the yard outside was crowded too. During the opening prayer the sky grew darker and darker. Thunder rolled, and the clouds turned that menacing hue that forebodes hail. All of a sudden, Blumhardt calmly departed from the fixed track of the liturgy with the words, "Loving God, if you mean to punish us for our sins and undo the blessing of our harvest, we would not dare to plead with you against that. But surely you will be gracious enough to let us hear your word undisturbed." He then continued with the liturgy. I felt like hiding under the pew at such audacity, but lo and behold, it suddenly became lighter, and in a few minutes the sky was blue again and the sun shining.

Things did not always turn out so well for Blumhardt. Still, he was not afraid of receiving a negative response to a request, but saw the hand of God in everything. "Faith has pulled us through again," he would remark whenever a predicament was solved. He expressed this in a letter to Barth:

> My theory about illness is biblical. It took root in me through the constant reading of the Bible from childhood on. Later, I was given repeated intimations of its truth, and these were strengthened and raised to certainty by experience. My supreme maxim is this: Everything comes from God.
>
> Faith is a duty. Most sick men would rather walk ten hours than search their consciences or bend their knees. But that is unbelief, and if it is connected with a bad conscience, it is sin. The Gospel does not say anywhere that we ought to seek God's help in some devious or roundabout way.

Blumhardt could never understand one objection that several of his critics raised – that is, their claim that the confidence with which he prayed for physical ills to be taken away violated the principles of patience and resignation. He believed that God is always inclined to help us, if only we implore him earnestly enough. If we fail to do so, it is we who prevent his coming to our aid. Asking God for something does not exert pressure on him, for true prayer is prepared for a negative answer. As he put it: "Asking calls for faith and patience. Faith expects everything, patience nothing."

Certainly he detested the sort of prayer that presses God for one's own desires, and he warned against the long, passionate prayers popular in some circles. At the same time he could admit, "I have noticed that something not attained by asking for it once or twice may yet be given when prayed for a third or fourth time." He often took the apostle Paul's example – "three times" (2 Cor. 12:8) – and then assumed that God did not want to grant that particular request.

Behind the objection to Blumhardt's prayers for healing was the notion that truly a devout person would prefer to model exemplary patience, than be freed from suffering. Blumhardt respected the forbearance of people who quietly endured suffering for years, but he questioned any sort of "patience" that forbade praying for help. "It is much easier," he once said, "to slip into a wrong kind of submission to God's will than to draw the bolts that hold back God's help." Another time he put it even more bluntly, "Why should we want to suffer and not want to believe? When we look closely at what lies behind it, we will find that most people would rather suffer than repent." To a sick woman he wrote, "Beware of showing off your patience. What is demanded of you is faith, and if you ignore that, you will make yourself guilty." It is insincere to endure only, and refuse to ask for relief.

The poor, misguided people – will they never recognize the delusion which they serve when they talk to God of their patience? I will not deny that a person's inner life may improve through suffering. But it is also common knowledge that people afflicted with chronic illnesses often become more, not less contrary, headstrong, self-willed, grumpy, and impatient. Clearly, in most cases people lack that which they need most: God's direct intervention.

It was not only Blumhardt's irritation at hypocritical attitudes that sparked this outburst, but compassion for humanity and confidence that even the most threadbare relationship to God can be completely restored. In short, Blumhardt was confident that God *would* send help if he were only asked.

Dr. de Valenti, a cleric who had demanded that Blumhardt leave the treatment of mentally ill people to physicians, said he should restrict his activity to pastoral care, to "instruction, rebuke, and comfort." In his reply, Blumhardt explained how he arrived at his simple faith, especially in his care of the mentally ill:

> As a rule, application of the spiritual pressure you recommend only serves to excite the sick, often increasing their agitation to a veritable frenzy. Instruction, rebuke, and comfort are least helpful at the beginning. When asked for advice, I forbid relatives to use these three approaches. And in my own counseling, I only use them cautiously and in moderation. What is really needed is something that

must come from above. Otherwise, there can be no help – only false "help" that does more harm than good.

But how can we receive this gift from above? Indeed, the gates of heaven, which at one time stood open, now seem to be closed. There is so much prayer, but how little it achieves! How often people come and say almost despairingly that all their praying changes nothing.

According to the New Testament, God wants to offer his gifts through human instruments. The gospel is to be proclaimed by servants of God, ambassadors for Christ, and these messengers are to bear spiritual gifts and powers for the church. That is why the apostles were endowed with exceptional power, both to preach and to heal.

Christianity knows absolutely nothing of this anymore. Hence all the despair in face of misery, and the devious means many try. Hence, too, the plight medical science finds itself in: it is expected to replace by its skills what the servants of the gospel ought to provide but have long since forfeited. In this case, medical science is to be commended for having labored far more faithfully than the servants of the gospel, in spite of the unbelief it professes as a body. Especially in the case of mental illness, most pastors cut a pathetic figure alongside physicians.

But is there no hope for change? In my fight with powers of possession I dared to do more than a pastor is accustomed to. I put no trust in myself, and credited myself no more than any other pastor. But

I approached the matter as a servant of the gospel, who does have a certain right to ask God for something.

I soon came to see, though, that the gates of heaven were not yet completely open to me, and I felt like giving up in discouragement. Still, the sight of sick people who could see no prospect of help anywhere gave me no peace. I remembered Jesus' words: "Ask, and it will be given to you; seek, and you will find; knock, and the door will be opened to you." I thought: If through unfaithfulness, unbelief, disobedience, negligence, and indolence the church and its servants have lost the power to drive out demons, Jesus might have been thinking of just such times of spiritual famine when he told the parable in Luke 11:5–8:

> Suppose one of you has a friend who comes to him in the middle of the night and says, "My friend, lend me three loaves, for a friend of mine on a journey has turned up at my house, and I have nothing to offer him," and he replies from inside, "Do not bother me. The door is shut for the night; my children and I have gone to bed; and I cannot get up and give you what you want." I tell you that even if he will not provide for him out of friendship, the very persistence of the request will make him get up and give him all he needs.

I could relate to that man standing at the door at midnight. Even though God was my friend, I was not worthy to obtain anything from him. Still, I could not bear to give up on a member of my congregation. I kept knocking. Some say that amounted to tempting God and was impudent, spiritually presumptuous, and fanatical. But I could not leave my guest standing at the door. I had to be patient for a long time, but in the end God did accede to my request. Was it wrong of me to pester him so?

And what was the result of my entreaties? The unwilling friend in the parable did not say, "Just go away. I myself will bring your guest what he needs – I don't need you for that." Rather, he gave the three loaves to his friend to use them for the guest at his discretion. It stands to reason that there was something left over, for the guest would be unlikely to consume all three loaves at once. By that I mean to say that God did indeed confer power on me, particularly to overcome demon possession. I was given this power in order to free a member of my congregation who was severely tormented by the devil, and who was entrusted to my care.

I used the three loaves and had some left over. Still, the supply was small, and new guests arrived, who came because they knew I cared for their needs and would take the trouble to approach "my slumbering friend" for further handouts at inappropriate hours. Each time I received what was needed, with some to spare.

How could I help it if now the wretched and tormented came running to me? Was I to become hard and say, "Why do you always come to my house?

There are many other houses in town – big, roomy ones – go there?" They would have replied, "Good sir, we have been there already, and they told us that they could not feed us and could not be troubled to get what was needed from a friend. Can you get us something to eat, for we are hungry and hurting?" What was I to do? Their distress touched my heart. Even though it was a bother for me, I went again and again to get more loaves. I was given them many times, much more quickly than at first, and with more left over. Of course, this bread is not to everybody's taste. Now and then, for whatever reason, someone leaves my house hungry.

In this way, Blumhardt defended his actions but reproached his fellow "servants of the gospel" for showing so little interest in wanting to recover the gifts of apostolic times. He was convinced that what was given to him was meant to show that God wanted to give new courage and power to everyone ready to pray for a better time:

Jesus says, "I have authority from my Father to forgive sins, and those whom I forgive are forgiven." What the Lord did, ought to continue, for everything he did as a man shall be done by other human beings until the end of days. The Father authorized him, and he authorized others. He said to the disciples, "As my Father has sent me, so I send you." Thus his disciples could say to repentant sinners as decisively as Jesus himself did, "Take heart, your sins are forgiven." And what is to shake our conviction that this power remains in force for those proclaiming the good news today – that they, too, should have authority to forgive sins?

Some people find it hard to accept that God should listen to a particular person's intercession more than to that of others – especially their own – and that God is willing to be approached through an intermediary. James 5:14 gives insight: "Is any among you sick? Let him call for the elders of the church, and let them pray over him." James did not regard miraculous help as a gift to the individual, but rather to the entire church. As Blumhardt often pointed out, the significance of the power he had been granted went far beyond his work as a pastor or healer, and far beyond Möttlingen:

> If someone asks whether everything God does through me is tied to my person or can be copied, I must answer that something has indeed been given to me as a result of the fight – and I doubt everybody can suddenly have it in the same manner. But I am convinced that it must become widespread, and that we should ask for the original powers of the gospel to be fully restored. For the time being, though, what has happened through me shows that we are justified in pleading for a renewal.
>
> But until the heavens open up, that renewal will not take place. It is wrong to think that believing is all that is needed to experience apostolic times again.

No, those powers can only slowly be won back. Christianity's faithlessness and apostasy over two thousand years have aroused the Lord's disfavor as well as an upsurge of satanic powers. The first thing that is needed is the conversion of Christendom.

Blumhardt never doubted that this renewal would come, or that it was worth fighting for. He had tasted victory, and through him many others had too. What God gave one village through one man who turned to him, he wants to give the entire world. Möttlingen's triumph over darkness should give us courage to face our own demons, and hope to expect greater things to come.

We are a dehydrated people. Nothing will quench our thirst and end the drought but God pouring out his spirit once again. Only a fraction of the promise was fulfilled at the time of the apostles. Must it not now be fulfilled on a larger scale? This stream of the Spirit will come – let us await it with confidence. The thirst is almost killing us, and people are deteriorating both inwardly and outwardly. But now, because we need this spirit, God will give it again.

THE AUTHOR

Friedrich Zuendel (1827–1891), the Swiss pastor, author, and essayist, is best known for his landmark biography of Johann Christoph Blumhardt. First published in Germany in 1880, it has been re-issued dozens of times and still remains in print.

OTHER TITLES

ACTION IN WAITING
CHRISTOPH FRIEDRICH BLUMHARDT
AFTERWORD BY KARL BARTH

Grasp the joy of losing yourself in service to God and others. Blumhardt, in his quest to get to the essentials of faith, burns away the religious trappings of modern piety.

LIFT THINE EYES
CHRISTOPH FRIEDRICH BLUMHARDT

Blumhardt's prayers and the corresponding Bible passages bespeak a certainty in God's nearness; the peace that flows from them comes from an unshakable conviction that his kingdom is indeed on the way. Offers a wellspring of hope we can turn to again and again.

SEEKING PEACE
NOTES AND CONVERSATIONS ALONG THE WAY
JOHANN CHRISTOPH ARNOLD

Seeking Peace expores many facets of humankind's ageless search for peace. It plumbs a wealth of spiritual traditions and draws on the wisdom of some exceptional (and some very ordinary) people who have found peace in surprising places.

THE EARLY CHRISTIANS
IN THEIR OWN WORDS
EBERHARD ARNOLD

A topically arranged collection of primary sources that provides a guide and yardstick for Christians today. Marked by their stark simplicity and revolutionary fervor, these writings will stun those lulled by conventional Christianity.

FREEDOM FROM SINFUL THOUGHTS
J. HEINRICH ARNOLD

Sensitive and encouraging advice for coming through the universal struggle of temptation and unwanted fantasies.

THE VIOLENCE OF LOVE
OSCAR ROMERO
FOREWORD BY HENRI J.M. NOUWEN

In Romero's words we encounter a man of God humbly and confidently calling us to conversion and action. Those who let his message touch them will never see life in the same way again.

DISCIPLESHIP
LIVING FOR CHRIST IN THE DAILY GRIND
J. HEINRICH ARNOLD

A collection of thoughts on following Christ in the nitty-gritty of daily life. Includes sections on love, humility, forgiveness, leadership, community, suffering, salvation, the kingdom of God, and much more.

THE PLOUGH PUBLISHING HOUSE

To place your order, phone, write, or visit our website:

USA: Route 381 North, Farmington PA 15437
Phone: 1-800-521-8011 **Fax:** 724-329-0914

UK: Darvell Bruderhof, Robertsbridge, East Sussex, TN32 5DR
Phone: +44(0)1580 88 33 44 **or** 0800 018 0799

www.plough.com